MW01441032

CEREMONIES OF SACRED LIFE. Copyright © 2022 T.S. Valenzuela. All rights reserved. Printed in the United States of America. No part of this book may be used or reproduced in any manner whatsoever without written permission of the author.

FIRST EDITION

www.inthedivine.com

ISBN – 13: 978-0-9848276-2-6

CEREMONIES OF SACRED LIFE

Secrets of the Psychedelic Medicine Teachers

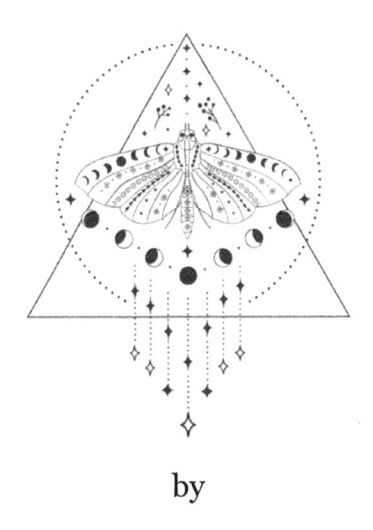

by

Theresa S. Valenzuela

in Service to

The Divine Mother

Contents

PREFACE	i
Chapter 1: The Basics	**1**
What We're Talking About	7
DMT is The Divine Mother is DMT	9
Listening Deeper	11
Chapter 2: Becoming En-Light-ened	**15**
The Human Energy System	*16*
Multiple Bodies	17
Cosmic Influences	18
Your Thoughts Create Your Body	20
The Space-Time Continuum	21
Hormones Are Communication Vehicles	23
Becoming Oneness	*24*
Chapter 3: How the Medicines Work	**30**
Compassion	33
Wounded Healers	34
Intentions vs. Prayers	38
Staying Present	42
Ceremonial Hive Mind	43
Set, Setting & Protection	45
Entities	48
Qualities of Experience	51
Chapter 4: The Great Karmic Balance	**54**
Intuition & Free Will	57
Growth & Expansion	62

1st Chakra Issues	65
Bathe Your Mind Before Ceremony	68
Perils & Pitfalls of Ceremony Circles	71

Chapter 5: The Celestial Information Superhighway — **77**

Our Celestial Family	*78*
The Endocannabinoid System	78
The Cannabis Industry	85

Chapter 6: Cosmorgasmic Energy — **92**

Considering Abstinence	93
Sexual Projections	95
Erotic Body Prayer	98

Chapter 7: Before & During Ceremony – Practical Tips — **102**

Before Ceremony	*102*
The Ceremonial Journal	102
Dietas	103
Integration	105
Your Support System	106
Planning Ahead	107

During Ceremony	*109*
Safety	109
Focusing Your Intentions & Prayers	111
Distractions	112
Expectations	114
Sailing Through Rough Passages	115
Purging	116
How to Know If The Dosage is Correct	117
Music	119
Talk Circle	120

Chapter 8: After Ceremony — **122**

How to Live an Intentional Life — *122*
  Own Your Stuff — 124
  Considerations For Your Loved Ones — 126
  Taking 3-D action — 129
  Putting It All Together — 131

Chapter 9: Blessings to You — **134**

Resources — **137**

  Shielding Technique — 137
  Food Prayers — 141
  Ceremonial Journal Questions — 143
  Ceremonial Journal Set-Up — 144
  How to Trust & Master Your Intuition — 149
  How to Start a Prayer & Meditation Practice — 156
  Psychedelic Integration Coaching — 159

Glossary of Terms — **161**

Acknowledgements — **170**

Author Biography — **172**

CEREMONIES OF SACRED LIFE

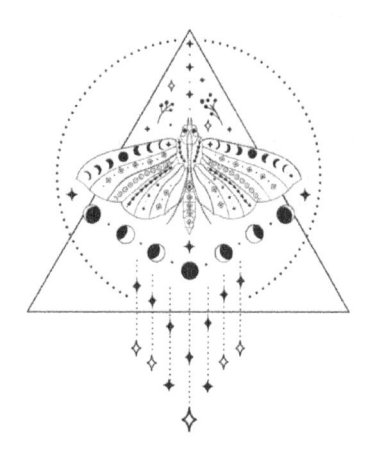

PREFACE

This is a book with practical tips for being a sovereign human being. It's a workbook and manual for navigating the sacred medicines before, during and after ceremony. If you're reading these words, you've been called here by the Divine Mother.

I'm a psychic and medium, and I've been working with sacred medicines, beginning with *ayahuasca* for about a decade now.

Ayahuasca is a tea that's been brewed since before recorded history in the Amazon, to enter alternate dimensions through shamanic work. It's primarily used for mind, body and spirit healing and for connecting to the divine and to the natural world. Ayahuasca is a revered sacred plant medicine who has a consciousness that connects with humanity. She is one of many entheogenic substances from across the globe, who are here to guide, teach and heal us. "Entheogen" comes from the Greek word *entheos*, meaning "god within" or "divinely inspired." An entheogen is a substance that allows one to experience an undeniable connection to a higher power.

I use the words "medicine," "sacrament," "psychedelic" and "sacred medicine" throughout this book to describe any of the entheogenic, hallucinogenic plants, animal products and fungi that have been ingested for healing and in shamanic and religious ceremonies throughout the world since before recorded history. Many indigenous cultures still weave entheogens into the fabric of their lives, including throughout pregnancy and childhood. Not all these cultures use the sacred medicines only in the ceremonial way that I refer to in this book, as every lineage takes a different approach.

To date, I've sat in seven different group medicine circles in the United States, with facilitators from the United States, Peru, Brazil and Columbia. I've experienced various traditions, including the Santo Daime Church, Shipibo, First Nations sound healing and more. I've delved into bliss and grief and learned multiple layers of the body-mind and how to communicate interdimensionally. I've worked with *ayahuasceros* to prepare the ayahuasca "tea" and I've done healing on ceremony participants, but I'm not here to be an *ayahuascera* or *curandera*. I leave that work in the capable hands of those from many different cultures who've dedicated their lives and hearts to that path.

(To clarify, an ayahuascero/a is someone who prepares ayahuasca and who may or may not also be a curandero/a - a trained healer experienced at offering healing at all levels – physical, mental, energetic and spiritual. Please see the Glossary of Terms for further definitions.)

Also, while I was a senior guardian in my main medicine circle, I'm not an "ayahuasca expert." I've done a ton of research on the psychedelic medicines, but there are many people who have decades more experience than I have. There are countless lineages I've never experienced, and much I don't know and never will. And that's how it should be. The sacred medicines communicate with us, but we aren't here to be "experts" about them. We're here to receive guidance from them as they connect us to God/source consciousness. If anyone tells you they're an ayahuasca or sacred medicine "expert," I'd ask for my money back and run quickly in the opposite direction.

Most people experience the "voices" of the sacred teachers as distinct from each other. The "spirit" of ayahuasca is most often experienced as a feminine voice, hence the moniker "Divine Mother" or "Grandmother." The Divine Mother has asked (i.e., commanded) me to write this book for Her, despite my reluctance to do so. I have a degree in creative writing, I've published a novel and I've been writing professionally for almost 30 years but writing about the psychedelic medicines was never on my radar. This book is channeled from the Divine Mother and not a book that deconstructs psychedelic medicines from the Western scientific model. There are bounteous books on the market that deconstruct ayahuasca and other sacraments from the scientific, cultural and healing point of view.

Why another book on the sacraments? I can only answer that creating this book is the desire of the Divine Mother at this dangerous time in history. Planet Earth is in jeopardy and the ultimate apex predators, the human beings who endangered the planet in the first place, are now also endangered from the

Preface

pandemic-fear-event that started in 2020. More people are coming to the sacred teachers for guidance and the Divine Mother feels the wisdom isn't being heard or applied by those who come for guidance.

She wishes you to understand that you are sovereign, meaning you alone have supreme power and authority over yourself, your thoughts and your actions. You were born with a direct line from your heart and mind to the divine, which you can tap into at any time. This connection can be accessed through a regular prayer and meditation practice as well as through the sacred medicines. Personal sovereignty begins with trusting your intuition, and your intuition comes directly from the divine. Without personal sovereignty you're always at risk to be manipulated by powerful forces who seek to control you via fear and darkness. The Divine Mother is here to show you a path to the light.

Why did She choose me to communicate her guidance through this book, and not an actual sacred medicine facilitator? I'm not completely sure, but I've learned the hard way that when the Divine Mother commands you to do something, you ignore it at your own peril.

I begin this project and benediction in alignment with the Divine Mother. This is no small task, as She has required that each word be channeled from Her and written in a state of prayer and high vibration from me, her scribe. While writing, I've been doing regular rituals, prayers, purifications and reflections and taking extreme care with my diet of food, people, media and thoughts. In case you were wondering, no, it's not all fun and games over here...

My deepest desire is that I remain in the light and in highest service to Her and to *you* as you receive Her message through me.

Blessings,

Theresa Schlee Valenzuela

2022

CHAPTER 1: THE BASICS

I'm terrified, in a big round room and people are starting to vomit. Loudly. It's freaking me out. What the hell am I doing here?

That's about thirty minutes into my first ayahuasca ceremony and at the end of it, I swore I'd never return. Three weeks later I was back for my second ceremony and the rest is history.

I came to ayahuasca after going to fifteen different healers and doctors over five years to get an answer for what was wrong with me. I received a diagnosis in 2018, six years after my 1st ayahuasca journey, when I finally had health insurance and was able to go to a sleep clinic. After three sleep clinic studies I learned that the official diagnosis for the chronic illness I'd been living with is idiopathic hypersomnia. *Idiopathic* means "no known cause," so idiopathic hypersomnia means there's something wrong with how your body processes sleep, but medical science has no idea what it is.

Not. Very. Comforting.

This is the definition from the National Institute of Neurological Disorders and Stroke:

> Hypersomnia is characterized by recurrent episodes of excessive daytime sleepiness or prolonged nighttime sleep. Different from feeling

tired due to lack of or interrupted sleep at night, persons with hypersomnia are compelled to nap repeatedly during the day, often at inappropriate times such as at work, during a meal, or in conversation. These daytime naps usually provide no relief from symptoms. Patients often have difficulty waking from a long sleep and may feel disoriented. Other symptoms may include anxiety, increased irritation, decreased energy, restlessness, slow thinking, slow speech, loss of appetite, hallucinations, and memory difficulty. Some patients lose the ability to function in family, social, occupational, or other settings... Some people appear to have a genetic predisposition to hypersomnia; in others, there is no known cause. Typically, hypersomnia is first recognized in adolescence or young adulthood.

The first hypersomnia episode I can remember, happened when I was 19 years old. The episodes didn't become debilitating until I weaned my son from breastfeeding in 2007. That's when all hormonal hell broke loose in my body, I got divorced and lived like a zombie single mom, raising my son and feeling suicidal three times a year from sleep deprivation until I got a diagnosis. The diagnosis helped me feel sane and not like I was just an overly emotional, certifiably insane insomniac. Insomnia is a mostly emotional condition that is usually relieved by good sleep habits and diet and lifestyle changes. Idiopathic hypersomnia is basically unfixable insomnia. The diagnosis helped me stop feeling suicidal, but I wasn't the type of person who feels comfortable with pharmaceutical drugs. I prefer to stick to whole foods and natural remedies, so it took about nine months after the diagnosis to start taking the prescribed pharmaceutical medicine, which I now take in a very small dosage, only as needed to function as a normal human.

To say I was desperate when I showed up at the door of ayahuasca in 2012 is putting it mildly. Without health insurance, sleep tests were out of reach, and after twenty-five years or so studying personal growth, human potential and spirituality, I held a firm but arrogant belief that I could heal myself. I have much more respect for Western medical science now than I did back then.

Various doctors had already offered me antidepressants like Halloween candy, but I knew that was never going to work for me long term, so ayahuasca was going to open some kind of door or I wasn't going to live to see my son grow up. I'd hoped that ayahuasca could give me answers or advice I couldn't find anywhere else. At thirty minutes into my first ceremony when it seemed like the whole room started violently purging, I wanted to run but had nowhere to go. I honestly believed that all other doors to hope in my life were closed and ayahuasca was all that was left for me.

Because I'm a nerdy writer, I've journaled after every one of my sacred medicine ceremonies, so I have extensive notes on all my experiences, realizations and lessons. But this book isn't my autobiography, so I'll keep my story brief. I came to ayahuasca to heal my brain and I ended up being called into service by the Divine Mother. Others are being called into service as well. As I mentioned in the Preface, this book is Her guidance to you, channeled through me.

After sitting in a few ceremonies, it occurred to me that I could *never* be a guardian. Guardians are experienced participants, chosen by the facilitator to be of service to the group. In most circles, the guardians are under the influence of the sacred medicine - in an altered state - while being of service to the participants. They're the go-to people for all aspects of the ceremony, including setting up participants in their spot for the night, emptying purge buckets, helping people to the bathroom, cleaning up the occasional overwhelming mid-ceremony poop purge, calming participants down if they're struggling, as well as setting up and taking down the ceremonial room. They also assist the facilitator with anything needed, help to prepare and offer the medicine and generally keep things flowing smoothly. Guardians can also be responsible for cooking and cleaning the kitchens and bathroom as well as the more fun and magical work of offering songs and healing throughout the ceremony.

At the beginning of my work with ayahuasca, being a guardian was unimaginable to me because I could barely sit up straight through the whole ceremony. I didn't take a second dose for almost three years and have only taken a third dose once. After that one-time third dose, I felt like I was being whirred around relentlessly in a cosmic blender with no "off" button. I don't plan on doing a third dose again any time soon...

As my ayahuasca journey unfolded over the years, my psychic abilities expanded. I've been a medium since I was a little girl, but I didn't realize it until the end of my first ayahuasca ceremony. As the sacrament was wearing off, I had a vision of a small indigenous woman standing in front of me. As she "talked" to me, I got the sense that her voice was the same one that had been guiding me throughout the ceremony and the same voice I'd been hearing in my head since I was a little girl. Somehow, I "knew" that the voice I'd been hearing inside my head for most of my life, belonged to the indigenous woman standing in front of me.

I said, "Oh my god, you're real?"

She replied, "Of course I'm real! I've been talking to you your whole life!"

I remembered that every time I'd seen a psychic, they said something to the effect of, "Who's that little, mean indigenous woman with braids who's insisting on communicating with you?"

In 2004, when I was pregnant for the first time, my baby girl died when I was eight and a half months pregnant. As you can imagine, it was a cataclysmic event in my life. My daughter's death changed my world, and it was the beginning of the end of my marriage. My husband at the time and I found out she'd died in the womb, and we ended up at the hospital the next day to induce labor. We had planned a home birth, so the hospital was the last place on the planet I wanted to be, but because of California laws, since she was already dead, the coroner would've had to come to our house to confirm the death and issue a death certificate. That was just a teeny bit too much reality for me at this most traumatic moment of my life, so the hospital was the better option.

While I was in labor, I "saw" a small indigenous woman who "told" me how to handle the labor. She gave me clear instructions, which turned out to be great advice for the situation. Sometime later, I was telling my mother about my visions during my daughter's birth and what the psychics had told me over the years and my mother said, "I think that's my grandmother! She was very mean, and she scared me. She was a medicine woman and the midwife of her community."

When I saw the vision of the indigenous woman in my first ayahausca ceremony in 2012, all the visions and messages and my mother's stories came together. I understood then that my *abuelita*, my great-grandmother, was the one who'd been communicating with me since I was little. Mind you, I wasn't concerned enough about these communications to talk to anyone during my childhood, because it seemed completely normal to me. It wasn't until my late 30s that I decided to talk to people about the voices they heard in their head too, and that's when I learned in some awkward moments that no one else was having the same experiences I was.

At the moment in my first ceremony when I saw my abuelita, I'd decided I'd had enough of ayahuasca and wasn't planning on ever coming back.

My abuelita said, "Oh yes, you're coming back. You'll come back and you'll take your medicine." And the rest, as I said, is history.

Somehow, I found the strength to be open to the guardian path and aside from raising my son, it's been the most challenging and rewarding job of my life. I'm eternally grateful to have been chosen for this deeply reverent sacred service.

As my sacred medicine life progressed, my abuelita became my touchstone. Ayahuasca opened the doors of perception to alternate dimensions and my abuelita was my guide. I've strengthened my psychic abilities over the years, and I talk to dead people daily. Whatever you may think when you read that, it feels completely normal to me. It's hardwired into the framework of what I am.

What We're Talking About

All living things have a unique energy signature and wisdom contained within them. Shamans through the ages have learned to tap into this energy signature in order to work with natural substances for healing. Psychedelic medicines are no different, except they hold within them the ability to alter human consciousness and communicate wisdom by connecting to receptors within the human body. In a sense, they "teach" us by connecting us to god consciousness.

There are many types of sacred medicine spirit teachers used throughout the world since before recorded history. A few better-known examples are the Amazonian *kambo* frog and the *bufo*/cane toad native to the Sonoran desert; both of whose secretions create a psychoactive effect. There's also *iboga*, a small African shrub whose bark is used ritually, ayahuasca, *huachuma* (or the colonial name San Pedro), cannabis plant and *peyote* cactus, as well as certain psychoactive mushrooms and fungi.

Sacred medicine energy is interdimensional, which is why people are visited by ancestors, spirit animals, the Celestial Beings and other entities in ceremony. This concept is broader than the conscious mind can conceptualize, so if you haven't experienced some type of interdimensional experience at a sacred medicine ceremony, you're just going to have to trust me here.

Sacred medicines help you tap into frequencies that are different than those required for your normal binds to reality. The medicines help you shift out of rigid ideas of yourself and your relationship to the cosmos. They allow you to travel a sacred bridge between earth and divinity and tap into a higher version of yourself, free of your ego aspect. When you allow their wisdom to move through you, you become a living example of what's possible with compassion and enlightenment. As you live with more light, you broadcast that light out to your loved ones, your community and as an extension, to the planet itself.

DMT IS THE DIVINE MOTHER IS DMT

The visions and messages that arise in ceremony are often accompanied by lights, colors and sacred geometrical patterns, which can be triggered by *N,N-Dimethyltryptamine* (DMT), mescaline, psilocybin and other compounds that exist within the psychedelic medicines. DMT is also present in the pineal gland and throughout the body (endogenous). While no one knows the complete truth of exactly how these compounds link with the brain, current scientific theory around ayahuasca and other psychedelics is that they stimulate, suppress, and/or modulate neurotransmitter activity in the brain. The specific neurotransmitter systems they influence are related to their unique chemical structures.

There's also debate in medicine circles about whether the lights, colors and geometrical shapes most people see while on the psychedelic medicines are a distraction from the spirit guidance or whether they're the guidance itself. DMT, mescaline, psilocybin and other psychoactive substances "turn on" the lights, colors and shapes, which are different than clear visions and communication from entities, angels, ancestors, animals, etc. They can all be happening at the same time, but for the purposes of this discussion, let's keep them separate.

The Divine Mother wants you to understand that these lights, colors and shapes are a coded, cosmic light language, communicated directly to your cells via activated DMT and other psychoactive substances. They're not just a distraction from the

The Basics

"real" information you're meant to receive in ceremony. That's why you don't see those lights, colors and shapes during your normal, waking life. While under the influence of psychedelic medicines, you have direct access to source consciousness as it communicates to you through a coded language of light. It's one of the reasons why focusing on your intentions during ceremony is so important. As you stay focused, this coded light language facilitates healing and expanded awareness inside of you, based on your intentions. Yes, it still works without intentions, but imagine the expanded blessings you can receive if you remain present to your intentions while you receive this cosmic light!

Later in the book I'll discuss how the vibration accompanying psychedelic phenomena is cosmic, orgasmic, ecstatic energy. This vibrating cosmorgasmic creation energy, which begins deep down in the light of cellular mitosis, is the energy that's downloaded into your cells through the activated psychedelic compounds. How cool is that?

What is cellular mitosis after all, but cellular reproduction, i.e., creation energy, i.e., sexual energy? Sexual reproduction is the highest drive in all life forms, and we can reduce that down to simple replication starting at the cellular level, i.e., cellular mitosis. What the Divine Mother wants you to know is that the coded light communication you receive through psychoactive substances is how the divine guidance lives inside of you after you return to your waking state. Therefore, you ALWAYS have a connection to this higher guidance, whether you're under the influence of sacred medicines or not. You can ALWAYS ask for guidance because it lives inside of you. ALWAYS.

Listening Deeper

As my first ever ceremony was finishing up, I got the message that ayahuasca emits the same tone as the core of the earth. Just as astrophysicists use the science of asteroseismology to "listen to" star frequency tones to determine the inner workings of stars, the core of the earth - which is mostly molten metal - emits its own tone and frequency. Ayahuasca and other sacraments are the means by which the energy of the planet, what some call Gaia or Pachamama, communicates to human beings. These ideas came to me with a sharp clarity and, I "knew" they were true as clear as day. Can I scientifically prove this myself? No, and yet it's still real for me and has made a huge impact on my life.

At the time I wasn't sure what to do with that information, but today I know that my understanding of how ayahuasca is connected to the core of the earth and the heart of Pachamama, is one of the reasons why the Divine Mother has called me to channel Her voice to you through this book.

By 2012, I'd been studying personal growth and human potential for 25 years. I studied Hawai'ian Huna, and I'm certified in Reiki, Neuro-Linguistic Programming, Hypnosis, Time Line Therapy™ and I had a "been there, done that" attitude. Being a life coach had become boring for me because it was mostly conscious mind discussion, and I sensed there was more to helping people transform, than just talking. My strong intuition was sensing great solutions for my clients, but because I hadn't yet embraced my psychic and medium abilities, I didn't know how to communicate that information effectively. After I began drinking ayahuasca, my psychic superpowers started to increase and solidify, so I knew I wanted to go deeper and further on the medicine path.

After many ceremonies, I got the crazy idea that I wanted to be a guardian after all. It looked like a difficult job with a lot of drama and responsibility and way outside of my abilities. So of course, I decided I had to know how to crack the code and be a GREAT guardian. Famous last words...

Being a ceremony guardian has been one of the most fulfilling roles I've had in my life, next to being mother to a magnificent human and a loving daughter-spirit on the other side. I've had the most beautiful and heart-opening experiences I never imagined were possible. I've also had the most disgusting (cleaning up piles of poop off of a semi-conscious, mentally unbalanced woman) and heartbreaking experiences as a guardian. In spite of how much emotional hurt I experienced when my main ayahuasca circle broke up (more in Chapter 5 on drama and unhealed emotional issues in ayahuasca circles), I wouldn't change any of my experiences for the world.

A few years into my ayahuasca service, the Mother showed me the power of the dark side. She showed me what dark energy looks like and compared it to light energy. From Her non-dualistic perspective, it's all just energy, but each energy yields different results. She showed me an experienced ayahuasca sister who enjoys working with dark energy. The Mother said, "This is your moment. You can choose the dark and live loudly like your sister or you can choose a quieter life and work behind the scenes, with the light. Which do you choose?"

My answer was immediate. "I choose the light."

"Alright," She said, "You'll be in my service going forward. I'll guide you from now on."

I continually surrender to the call of the Divine Mother and receive the psychedelic medicines for healing. In all of my ceremonies with different sacraments, I go into an altered state and receive messages from a variety of interdimensional beings. You can do this too. Since DMT is present throughout the body, it's already part of what humans are. That means your physiology is hard-wired to communicate interdimensionally and receive guidance from the sacred medicine allies who live with us on this planet.

Just sit with that for a moment...

Via the process of receiving transmissions of light and higher wisdom, I've also been initiated into damiana, cannabis, agave and sequoia so I can speak from the unique resonance and vibration of those teachers. I received an initiation directly from the giant sequoia trees right before a group of them burned in California, in the fall of 2021. There weren't many sequoias on the planet before, but between the California Sequoias lost in the Castle Fire of 2020 and the fire in the fall of 2021, their numbers have been decimated further. These great tree spirits are some of the oldest creatures on the planet and they told me they want to transmit their knowledge before they're killed off by our ignorance and mismanagement.

These initiations are part of the reason I was chosen by the Divine Mother to write this book and communicate Her messages to you at this unprecedented time in history, when human health and therefore planetary health is being manipulated by dark forces hellbent on using greed and fearmongering to pull humanity into fear and darkness. A population in fear is easy to control. Remember that.

Over the past decade, in addition to sitting in various group medicine circles, I've held solo ceremonies in the privacy of my own home. I've worked privately and received guidance from the energies of ayahuasca, psilocybin, cannabis, agave, damiana and huachuma. (I strongly advise against solo practice unless you're very experienced and you know unequivocally how to create and hold sacred space for others and yourself.)

In my continuing solo ceremonies, my ancestors and the sacred medicine spirit teachers communicate their messages to me, which I channel and transmit throughout my personal and business life. I'm most honored and deeply grateful to use this guidance to serve humanity to the best of my abilities.

CHAPTER 2: BECOMING EN-LIGHT-ENED

Desperation for healing is what brought me to ayahuasca in the first place, but not everyone comes to the medicine for healing. If you're asking yourself why anyone would drink a life-altering substance to take a big spiritual leap, then it's likely not for you at this time, which is perfectly fine. As a curandero once told me, "Ayahuasca is for everyone, but not everyone is for ayahuasca."

When people come to me with curiosity about psychedelic medicines, the two concerns I hear most are that they're either scared, to which I reply, "You should be," or they tell me they're afraid of vomiting/getting sick. While it's true that ayahuasca and other sacred medicines are purgatives, the purge is a benefit, not a drawback. It helps if you think of it as "getting well," instead of getting sick.

Purging from the stomach (vomiting) is only one of many pathways the sacraments use to relieve you of your negative delusions, blocks, fears, and resentments. You *want* that purging to happen! Better out than in, as they say. When we vomit outside of ceremony, it's often from food poisoning, the flu or another physical sickness. In sacred ceremony, getting sick is really getting well and it's best to experience it as a celebration of your enlightenment. The more blocks and negativity you release from your *Human Energy*

System, the better life you'll lead, which benefits everyone around you, the planet and society as a whole.

The Human Energy System

The Divine Mother wants you to know that the psychedelic medicines communicate directly to DNA, so healing is done at the molecular level, and this is how you become EN-LIGHT-ENED. It helps if you think of the human body less as a solid structure, a noun; and more of a verb - an interdimensional system that's in constant flux and flow. In other words, you're more than just a meat suit on a giant rock hurtling through space.

You may think it's solid, but the physical body is actually an interlocking energy system, a cosmic-body-mind that can communicate to and receive communication from multiple dimensions. I have a more accurate name for it – the Human Energy System. It's made up of your past, present and future, your intuition, feelings, emotions, values and beliefs and is created on a moment-to-moment basis by your thoughts.

It's possible to commune with divinity using your body and mind, and sacred medicines can facilitate that communication. I've seen repeatedly that ceremony participants have multidimensional healings that not only change their physical bodies in present time but heal ancestral trauma from the past as well.

As someone who talks to dead people and the Celestial Beings throughout my day, this makes complete sense, but I get that it may sound nonsensical to some. The sacred medicines invite you to open your mind to new ways of looking at your body and your world.

You are a body-mind connection, but that term is limiting because a connection implies two or more distinct parts, and this is not the case. Your mind *is* your body, and your body *is* your mind. Better said, the body is a metaphor for the mind. I cannot emphasize this enough. Your body is a metaphor for the state of your mind and your mind is far vaster than most people realize.

Your consciousness is connected to all consciousness on the planet and is affected by the energies of the cosmos at large. Science now recognizes that consciousness flows throughout the neural networks of the body. It's not localized solely within the grey matter inside your skull. Most people are aware that stress can cause disease in the body, and it's commonly accepted in the field of traditional medicine that stress affects your emotions and strong emotions affect the body. Is it such a stretch then, to accept that the body and the so-called mind are interlocking parts of a greater whole?

MULTIPLE BODIES

Christianity, the Hawaiian spiritual system, and the ancient East Indian philosophy of Ayurveda, among other philosophies, say the same thing: the human being as we know it is made up of more than one body. The famous psychologist Sigmund Freud defined it as id, ego and super ego. Christianity calls it body and soul and

Ayurveda refers to three different *doshas* or energetic qualities that shape the Human Energy System.

In the Hawaiian spiritual system, there are four bodies. Going from least to most matter density, we have the higher self/spiritual body, the emotional body, the mental body and the physical body. Life issues are easiest to heal when they're in the spiritual body. In other words, if we simply recognize in a moment of stress that we've forgotten we're one with source consciousness, we could simply re-adjust ourselves and feel better.

Generally, it doesn't happen like that. We feel a negative emotion about an issue and feel stress in the emotional body instead of letting the issue go. From there it goes to the mental body where we ruminate about it and feel anger, doubt and guilt or other negative emotions. If we hold onto those psychological complexes long term, they create blocks in our physical body. The medical establishment calls these blocks "stress-related illnesses."

Despite what we've learned from ancient philosophies, most people are still under the mistaken impression that their body is solid mass, and they ultimately have very little control over it, either because of genetics or a limiting belief that "it's just the way the body is."

Cosmic Influences

Whether or not you believe in astrology, I invite you to consider that the moon influences the oceanic tides and women's menstrual cycles as well. Research has shown that most women ovulate around the full moon.

As stated in the Science Advances Journal, Vol. 7, Issue 5, January 27, 2021

> In many marine species and some terrestrial species, reproductive behavior is synchronized with a particular phase of the lunar cycle (often full or new moon). This arrangement increases reproductive success by synchronizing the reproductive behavior of the individual members of a species. In light of this fact, it is of interest that the human menstrual cycle has a period close to that of the lunar cycle and that several older studies report a relation between the cycles. Women whose cycles approach the ~29.5-day period of the Moon have been reported to have the highest likelihood to become pregnant.

If you remember from biology class, hormones drive women's monthly cycles. If hormones drive women's cycles and the moon influences those cycles, following this line of logic it's easy to see that the moon influences us on a cellular level. If our moon, which is basically a speck of dust compared to say, Saturn, can have such a great influence on a woman that it can dictate what time of month she was able to create a new life (the greatest single act any life form is capable of) wouldn't the other planets - gargantuan, powerful bodies orbiting our galaxy - have an influence as well?

Even if you don't believe in astrology, when you consider the sciences of astronomy - (observing the cosmos), and astrophysics (using the theories of physics to analyze the cosmos), it's hard to ignore the direct evidence that the planets have an influence on us. We're an intrinsic part of the universe in a way that we don't directly experience through our five primary senses.

Your Thoughts Create Your Body

In a desperate effort to heal my chronic illness, I logged hundreds of hours of research and fifteen years of experience dealing with doctors and healers. The sacred medicines opened many doors of knowledge into my Human Energy System that far surpassed my research. I invite you to let the medicines help you peer closer than what you're accustomed to and see if you'll also receive deeper wisdom about your body than what science, society and cultural beliefs dictate.

What's the story you tell about your body? Your thoughts sing a symphony that solidifies into your body. What tune are you singing? Is it dissonant or melodic? Are you willing to entertain the possibility that your opinion of yourself is recorded in your body? When you receive the sacred medicines, they reveal the tune you've been singing with your thoughts. The question for you is, "What will you do with that song?"

For decades now, athletes have been using visualization techniques to improve their performance. Billie Jean King, Tiger Woods and Jack Nicklaus, as well as Olympic athletes, report using visualization as a mental practice alongside their physical practice. Studies have shown that the more athletes visualize the positive outcome they want, the more likely they are to get it. What this means to you as a multi-dimensional spiritual being is that your thoughts, perceptions, beliefs and expectations influence your life!

My novel, "Penelope In The Divine," is a fun, action-packed parable about some of the teachings in this book. Goba the Monk spends extensive time teaching the main character Penelope, about the Human Energy System. It's one of the first things he teaches her because it's the basis for spiritual ascension. If you believe you're a victim of life, of the forces around you, there's no way for you to become a self-actualized, enlightened individual, which is the invitation extended to you in this life on this planet. Recognizing that your actions, choices, thoughts and beliefs create the reality that you perceive as your "life," can help light your pathway toward enlightenment. As a 24/7 victim of external forces, you're powerless. As a being who can shift your body through your thought processes, you are empowered - unstoppable. These are typical messages that the sacraments reveal to you.

THE SPACE-TIME CONTINUUM

Another influence on your Human Energy System is the concept of time. Your body can be affected by past events, because you're holding onto trauma from the past, but your body can also be influenced by your attitude about the future.

Most indigenous cultures have shamans who work directly with their ancestral lineage and can access alternate dimensions to bring back information and healing from the spiritual realm to an individual or to the tribal community. Since the dawn of time, this work has been aided by the psychedelic medicines, who are expert teachers on time travel.

For a shaman, there's no difference between past, present and future. Even the Inca believed that time and space are one. Assuming this is true, where does the body, the Human Energy System reside? Right here, right now, or in a grander concept of space and time that we don't consider on a daily basis? If a shaman can use the sacred medicines to reach into the past and create healing to affect you in the future, where on the space-time continuum does the shaman reside? Where do you reside? Where is your body?

Whether or not you believe in past lives, consider that our bodies exist in more than just this moment, right here, right now. If our bodies are a composite of our past experiences, if they can be affected by the sacred medicines, can we truly state with 100% certainty that our bodies are only what we can see with our eyes or feel with our touch?

HORMONES ARE COMMUNICATION VEHICLES

Most people have at least a cursory familiarity with hormones and many women can feel the changes they evoke, especially during the menstrual cycle and menopause, but what exactly are hormones? I delved deeply into this question when I was ill and desperately seeking help and a diagnosis for my medical condition. Nothing healed my physical body so I did whatever I could to approach my physical issues from different perspectives. I researched hormones and translated the scientific speak into language a five-year-old could understand because that's how I felt when I read science articles!

What it came down to is hormones are communication vehicles. They simply carry communication from one receptor site to the next, based on a complex interplay of activities happening in the body as it maintains internal homeostasis. This is similar to how your body receives psychedelic medicine, which activates the molecular receptor sites in the body.

If our internal, cellular communication might be working improperly, doesn't it make sense that it can be reflected in our external communication as well? Is your physical state causing you to have strained relationships and stunted communication with your loved ones? Where does the body end and the mind begin? Where do external factors end, and internal factors begin? How does stress, which is an external event, "get inside" the body to cause a ruckus and create a stress-related illness?

The answer is there's no difference between "out there" and "in here." The human body and as it follows, health itself, is a vast web of consciousness affected by your thoughts and experiences. This could be good news or bad news, depending on how you look at it. Are you a victim or a creator? The sacred medicines will open your mind to questions like this, which can permanently alter how you perceive yourself. In case you were wondering, that's a *good* thing.

Chronic health issues are a sign that there are miscommunications happening somewhere within your Human Energy System. The Divine Mother wants you to know that if you have physical issues that you're bringing to ceremony to heal, having an open mind and expanded idea about what your body *really* is will help you receive and integrate the wisdom from the sacred medicines.

Becoming Oneness

Remember that you get what you focus on. Since most doctors within the American healthcare system focus only on dis-ease, that's all they're going to see. If you fall into the cracks between dis-ease and vibrant health (which happens if you have a chronic illness), most doctors don't know what to do with you.

Ayahuasca and other spirit teachers communicate with the parts of you that are outside of the conscious waking state that doctors and most healers see. You have an entire lifetime of rigid dealings with the physical, 3-D plane, which is why most of humanity needs an entheogenic substance applied to their cells to receive interdimensional messages and deeper healing, especially about health.

Ayahuasca, cannabis and psilocybin are all becoming more popular and more easily accessible today and this is no mistake or coincidence. The Divine Mother wants you to know that the sacred teachers are reaching more people now because planet Earth is in peril. Whatever headway we were making before the pandemic-fear-event started in 2020, has been reversed by the solidified fear collective that the planet is currently steeped in. This fear has strained our collective mental and emotional health and has caused people to create mountains more medical waste, food packaging and other trash than the planet can handle. She wants you to wake up to the horror this collective fear has created. Only with this knowledge can we change the situation. The time is now.

As people continue with medicine experiences, one of the most marked, consistent changes they make, no matter their culture or nationality, is becoming more environmentally aware; more conscious of living sustainably. Many people translate that energy into having a vegan diet and avoiding all animal products. While the gesture is lovely, it's important to understand that in many cases, a vegan diet relies on highly processed and packaged food, which create an environmental burden the same as concentrated animal feeding operations (CAFOs).

Having a vegan diet isn't a complete environmental solution the same as showing up to a ceremony with crystals doesn't make you more spiritually attuned. The Mother would like you to be aware that the external trappings of spirituality are not spirituality itself! If you want to be more mindful about what you eat, begin with prayer. All things exist as a frequency. No matter your dietary choices, unless you grow and prepare all your own food, you cannot know for certain if your food was raised and packaged with love and compassion. To raise the frequency of what you eat, bless anyone who had a hand in growing and creating the food on your plate, including yourself. Bless the animals, rodents, birds, lizards, insects and any other animals that were killed during the agricultural production of your food. Animals are sacrificed for our food, whether they're killed in the process of cultivating plant crops or killed directly for their flesh. Acknowledge that we merge with the souls of the sacrificed life forms. There's no getting around other living things dying for human food, so acknowledge it with awareness, deep reverence, prayer and gratitude. Please see the Resources section for food prayer examples.

As you progress along your sacred medicine path, understand that keeping a vegan diet, getting spiritual tattoos, doing more yoga and surrounding yourself with sage, palo santo and crystals, aren't solving your issues of en-light-en-ment outright. The only thing that can make you more enlightened is to continually take a laser sharp look into yourself and take stock of your humanity and how you treat your body, other humans, life on the planet and the planet itself.

The Divine Mother is one with source consciousness and facilitates communication between celestials and humans. Being able to communicate properly along these channels takes deep introspection, facing your fears and shadows and cleaning up messes you've made by generating enough courage to have hard conversations with your loved ones. It has nothing to do with how many crystals you own, or what tattoos you have on your body. It requires you opening your heart and taking responsibility for what you find there.

She is saying that many are missing the point of communication with the sacred medicine spirit teachers. The point, relatives, is ONENESS. From oneness comes the ability to recognize others as yourself and to treat them with the same level of compassion and kindness that you'd treat yourself. If you're not treating *yourself* with compassion and kindness, then that's where your work must begin.

Going to one ceremony after the other won't solve problems either. Unless you're consistently doing the homework that was assigned to you in ceremony, there's no point in returning. Save the dosages of the sacrament you crave for someone who's willing to put in the effort required to evolve. If you've been shown ways in which you've been selfish, for example, and you do nothing to fix your less than perfect behaviors, but decide the answer is to ingest more medicine to quell your day-to-day discomfort, think again.

Stay home and do your inner reflection and healing. Face your fears, anxieties and resistance and find ways to integrate and heal these issues before you return to your sacred medicine teachers.

The Divine Mother wants to be clear that in ceremony you will be shown your blocks to the light. Your job is to continue to remove those blocks. Without the ongoing inner-work and integration, taking more of the sacraments is a disrespectful waste of finite, natural resources and sacred wisdom. Many people show up to psychedelic medicine circles ill-equipped to integrate the visions, lessons and healings into day-to-day life. This is an unfortunate side effect of modern society.

In ancient times we lived in tribal settings where everyone had access to the tribal healer and integrating mystical experiences was weaved into the fabric of life. In modern times, most people travel to sacred medicine ceremonies and then travel right back home to their previous lives. Unless ongoing integration with the facilitator was part of the ceremony package, participants are left to themselves to translate and integrate what they experienced. This can create all kinds of problems! I'll give some specifics about how to make the most of your time with the medicine in Chapters 7 and 8, but for starters, one thing I recommend to everyone who asks me is to bring a journal to ceremony and write down your experience as soon as possible after the ceremony is closed. I usually write some notes before I go to sleep and then fill in the details the next morning before talk circle. I also continue to journal any thoughts about the ceremony as they come up in the following days.

Ceremonies of Sacred Life

In the Resources section, I share a simple journaling practice that's a wonderful way to link your unconscious mind (the part of you that received the visions) to your conscious mind (the part of you that operates your waking life). It's a valuable grounding tool to help you integrate and process the changes that are happening inside of you, so you can remain on the path of en-light-en-ment and moving toward oneness.

CHAPTER 3: HOW THE MEDICINES WORK

Psychedelic medicines have been used all over the world since ancient times, and they vary from culture to culture. No one knows exactly how long these sacraments have been in use, but over the past few hundred years, knowledge of the sacraments was eradicated by missionaries and colonizers who sought to dominate indigenous people and destroy their culture. This dismissal of indigenous culture and philosophy has contributed to worldwide ecological destruction and has replaced the reverence for communicating directly with the natural world for a hard-line adherence to left-brain scientific theory as the only means for acknowledging "truth" and validity.

Religion is "one size fits all." The same sets of principles are applied to anyone who follows the religion. Sacred medicines are different because they allow you to receive messages in a way that's unique to you and your current situation and physical and emotional constitution. They eliminate the middleman - the religious officiant - and allow you to communicate directly with divine energy, or God. This of course, is one of the reasons religious missionaries were threatened by psychedelic medicine use in indigenous cultures and abolished the knowledge as they violated the people.

Ceremonies of Sacred Life

Everyone who works with the sacraments has an opportunity to connect in a two-way conversation with higher consciousness. The ceremony facilitator is there as a guide, not necessarily to interpret for you the messages you receive. Most of the time, when you're under the influence of medicines, you automatically understand what you're being shown, so you don't *need* a middleman or a scientific study to interpret the wisdom for you. This is both a blessing and a curse, as it forces you to expand your awareness and believe in yourself and your intuition, rather than doubt it.

Working with the sacraments, I've learned how deeply interconnected everything is. It's a common theme in psychedelic medicines, and something that can't be proven by science as we know if. But it's the experience of connection that opens you up to living with compassion as you continue your journey of enlightenment. Even if you bring the most challenging, confusing situation into a ceremony, you have the potential to receive guidance around it and see how it fits into your life as a whole. Perceiving situations in an entirely new way is one of the mystical gifts the sacraments give you.

A few years back I was the victim of an online scam. Not only was I embarrassed that I fell for the scam in the first place, but it wiped out my bank accounts. The bank locked my accounts while they did an investigation and for almost 2 weeks, I had no way to pay for gas or groceries for myself and my son. When I made it back to ceremony, I was sure I'd be shown how evil the perpetrators of this scam were and how much they deserved to be punished, but surprisingly, the opposite happened.

The Divine Mother showed me that the people who were running the scam were just like me. They had families to provide for and bills to pay and had simply made the karmic-heavy choice of getting their livelihood from harming other people. If anything, I should have compassion for them and feel mercy toward them.

That was not at all what I wanted to hear! But it opened me up to see that there were greater forces at work than I could understand in my angry and humiliated state. In the end, that experience forced me to get clear about my finances. I was unemployed at the time, scared around 1st chakra/survival-level issues, and exhausted because of my sleep disorder. In my exhaustion, I'd missed some important red flags when this scam crossed my path, and I succumbed to it because I was in a weakened state. After this terrible predicament brought me to my knees in humility, I took a class on how to manage my finances and get out of debt. It turned my life around and I now consider myself a great money manager.

What ayahuasca helped me to do in this case, was to see my life experience from a god's-eye view. I saw the perpetrator of this crime as someone who lived in a harmful way, and they deserved my compassion much more than they deserved my hatred. It freed me from holding onto anger and hatred and gave me the opportunity to once again choose humility and love in the most challenging of situations. This is the type of wisdom that psychedelic medicine can offer to help you live in a more accepting and charitable way.

Compassion

The most repeated theme through every single sacred medicine ceremony I've attended is compassion: compassion for self and others. Compassion is the currency of enlightenment and it's the currency that all the sacred medicines use as they weave their magic inside the Human Energy System. In medicine circles this is also called "heart-opening." But what does that mean, exactly and why is it so important that it's infused within the wisdom of all sacred medicines?

No one knows the answer for certain, but the spirit teachers do reveal the divinity that resides within each one of us. Sacred medicines dwell within the temple of the spirit and they can reveal to you what your life can be like if you choose to live compassionately, with an open heart. Without fail, you'll be shown both the blocks and the doorways to your compassion. Passing through the doorway of compassion now and then is easy, especially after a heart-opening medicine ceremony, but living your life with compassion is something else entirely. It requires courage and faith, and will have you facing your deepest, darkest demons. This path isn't for the faint of heart.

The Divine Mother also wants you to know that humility is best when approaching the psychedelic medicines for guidance, because humility keeps you in a close resonance with their purity of communication. Stay humble and keep track of the visions around areas in your life that need healing and reflection.

The changes you need to make in order to live a compassionate life, won't necessarily be solved by ingesting more sacred medicines – that's the tricky part. I've seen many people wearing the garment of spiritual evolution after drinking some ayahuasca, without doing the internal processing and integration that will actually make them a better person. There's no shortcut here. No matter how experienced you are, the medicine will reveal your darkness to you without fail. It's up to you to actually DO something about it. Stay in alignment with your inner work and you cannot go wrong.

WOUNDED HEALERS

There are no exceptions to this rule, which is why we hear so often about facilitators and curanderos/as who are out of integrity in their work. There are many published stories about facilitators who take sexual advantage of their participants. As I mentioned previously, ecstatic, sexual energy is coded into the sacred medicines, so if you're working with someone who's out of their integrity, it can create an open space for sexual abuse and manipulation.

One of the most incredible ayahuasca journeys I've ever had was with a facilitator who poured powerful medicine and shared powerful music. He held ceremonies globally and created a space of deep healing and transformation wherever he went. He also had a reputation for becoming romantically involved with participants and was ultimately accused of sexual abuse by one of them.

I've also encountered facilitators and curanderos/as who hold impeccable space in ceremony but are deeply troubled in their day-to-day life and some are alcoholics and/or drug addicts. This may seem incongruous – how can someone be a great healer and be a deeply troubled human at the same time? It boggles the mind, but it's been happening since time immemorial, hence the well-known biblical phrase, "Physician, heal thyself."

The Divine Mother would like you to know that ayahuasca and other sacraments are not a cure-all. This is a free-will planet, and you're welcome to override celestial guidance, which is how someone can be a great healer with a deep connection to the sacraments, and yet still choose to abuse themselves and others. It's up to you to use the knowledge, love and insights you've been shown to remain in alignment with the light.

Many people come to ceremony and have a fairly easy time with the medicine. In other words, they don't feel like they're going to pass out and dissolve every time, like the more sensitive people do, myself included. I've seen these medicine people with a strong constitution develop a bit of experience with the sacred medicines, and then because they're healers of some sort in their daily lives, feel like it's their "job" to "hold space for others" in ceremony. But when it comes right down to it, they don't fix themselves because they're too busy with the notion that their job is to be of service to others and therefore, they deserve to hold a higher space in the medicine circle. This is power-hungry seeking from the ego, and it eventually gets revealed.

Thinking you're above other ceremony participants or that you don't need to do deep healing and integration because it's your "job" to "help" others, is a dangerous trap to fall into. Sooner or later, the sacrament and the Divine Mother will kick your ass.

I've seen those with powerful physical constitutions finally get slapped down by the Divine Mother with a terrifying psychedelic medicine experience and then stop coming to ceremony. Their arrogance is revealed to them, and they turn away instead of changing. I've also seen senior medicine people called out because of their dismissive attitude toward the participants and then never accept that feedback. They believe they're more evolved than the other participants and crave a position of authority because they feel they deserve it, since they're healers in their day-to-day life or have more overall experience with the sacraments. When they don't receive the position of authority they crave, they leave the circle. Some of them experience ongoing drama and trauma in their personal lives because they're codependent and trying to help others without helping themselves first. There's nothing more destructive than an egomaniac, out-of-balance healer. If you encounter someone like this, trust your intuition about how to deal with them and whether you should avoid them altogether.

I've seen others with addiction issues, continuously return to the psychedelic medicines without using the sacred wisdom they're given to heal their addiction. They go right from ceremony back to their drug of choice, in an endless loop of personal deceit and destruction. These behaviors divide ceremony circles and destroy lives.

For my part, the Divine Mother kicks my ass each and every time I go into ceremony. I'm sensitive on all levels and even small amounts of medicine, especially ayahuasca, will have me fighting to sit up straight and remain conscious. I still stay present to be of service as a guardian and to do the homework She assigns me. It's unpleasant to face my shadow, and arduous work, but everyone around me benefits from my inner reflection and elevation, and the same goes for you.

The Divine Mother wants you to know that your experience of the sacraments is a reflection of the leader creating the space. I know of a curandero who held a high vision for humanity and was loved by many. He was open and generous to anyone who needed the medicine and rarely said no. He committed his entire adult life to the healing arts and helped thousands of people over his whole career but couldn't help himself and heal his own addictions. As he became sicker over the years, he was often negative and unkind to those closest to him. The strength of his circle diminished until it was eventually dissolved by the addict energy he drew to him. There are stories like this all over the world – it's not a few isolated incidents.

The Divine Mother wants to be clear that ayahuasca and other sacraments need humans to transmit the sacred messages, and incredible healings can occur at the hands of imperfect facilitators. Please understand that no curandero/a is perfect, and no participant is perfect, yet until you have significant experience and are ready for solo ceremonies (which takes a while), guided circles are still the best way to receive the medicine. That's why it's important to go into a sacred ceremony fully prepared and why I recommend you always take responsibility for energetically protecting yourself. I'll talk about preparation in Chapter 7: Before & During Ceremony – Practical Tips.

INTENTIONS VS. PRAYERS

The Divine Mother wants you to know that surrendering to the sacraments allows your mind to open enough to allow changes to take place inside of you. These changes happen when you're open to a different perspective of the issues you bring to ceremony and that new perspective can only happen when you get out of your conscious mind and tap into greater universal wisdom, which the sacred teachers will help you do.

As you continue to spend time with the sacred teachers, your life will evolve and change. The changes may be subtle, drastic, or even cataclysmic. Much of that has to do with the intentions you bring to ceremony. Since the psychedelic medicines can mold to fit your current state of consciousness, it's highly recommended and beneficial to have an intention for each ceremony you attend, especially if you're new to the sacred medicine experience. An intention is a purpose or desire, which gives you two navigators for your consciousness – your mind plus the medicine. Intentions guide the powerful sacred medicine energy toward your growth and desires. That doesn't mean you're going to get exactly what you want, when and how you want it, but intentions will help move your life in the direction you want it to go.

Also, based on my experience and observation, I recommend you keep your intentions about yourself. Whenever I've seen someone come into ceremony with intentions to heal a loved one from cancer, for example, or to have their child make different life choices, they end up having an incredibly difficult experience. Someone else's healing is not up to you unless they've chosen you as their healer for an energy exchange. No one knows the higher good for someone else and for all you know, it may be part of someone's soul progression to go through a serious illness or destructive chapter in their life.

My brother died in 2020 after a prolonged and horrific battle with multiple sclerosis. It was heart wrenching to experience him debilitated for so many years. Yet when he communicated with me after he died, he showed me that from a soul level he was a powerful healer, and he wanted the debilitating physical experience in this lifetime so he could be an even better and more compassionate healer in his next life. There was no way I could have known that, and truthfully, it wouldn't have helped me feel less grief for him or miss him less. However, that was *his* path to choose. No amount of well-meant interdimensional sacrament interference on my part would have changed that.

If you desire healing for a loved one when you come to ceremony, instead of an intention, I invite you to offer a prayer that they remain in the highest light of consciousness and progress joyfully and in alignment on the path of their dis-ease (or something like that). Affirm a prayer for grace and awareness for them and acceptance and peace for yourself. You can also have an intention that you receive guidance on how best to support *their* soul's journey through the dis-ease. In this way, you honor their process and open yourself up to support them for the highest good of all concerned.

The same goes for healing the planet, shifting the mindset of a violent despot or healing conflict in a war-torn region. These are humongous issues for one person to take on with sacred medicines. The planet cannot be "healed" through your Human Energy System. But you can affirm a prayer that the violent despot will come into the light and ask for guidance for yourself so you may more do your part to achieve world peace. Ask for wisdom about how to communicate the planet's needs or how to organize politically to create awareness for your cause. Allow the sacred teachers to handle the healing and for their guidance on how you can do a better job of being a more productive, aware, helpful, environmentally conscious and compassionate human being, for the highest good of all concerned. Any shift you make toward the light will help the planet and humanity as a whole.

To make the most of your intentions and prayers, write them down in your ceremonial journal and keep them as simple and brief as possible. Keeping them brief helps you memorize them so they're easier to recall during any difficult passages you experience. Also, it's perfectly fine to ask for your lessons to be easy and gentle and to have fun during ceremony or in your life overall. You may not get what you want, but it doesn't hurt to ask!

A caveat about intentions is to consider that they may not be given to you in the way that you ask for them. To understand this better, I often use the metaphor of sedimentary rock layers. When you look at sedimentary rock, it's layer upon layer, from deep in the earth, all the way up to the surface. You cannot get to a deeper layer of the rock without moving through the upper layers – it's just not possible.

Intentions work in much the same way. If you bring a certain intention to ceremony, you may get clarity on it then and there, or you may be shown something you need to learn first, at an upper level, before you reach the deeper levels where the complete fulfillment of your desire lies. This is another reason why it's important to have an open mind and release expectations when working with the psychedelic sacraments.

When crafting intentions and prayers, bullet points are best. For example:

- Release my anger toward ...
- Heal my...
- Receive a great love in my life
- Manifest greater wealth

- Have fun!
- Prayers for my son and daughter
- Prayers for Uncle Joe & Aunt Lois

STAYING PRESENT

Staying present is an important part of having a fruitful experience in ceremony. When the sacrament kicks in, it's easy to feel lost in your thoughts. Staying present with your intentions is a good way to bring yourself back into the experience of the psychedelic medicine and out of spinning thoughts in your head. No matter what's going on around you, your best course of action is to stay present with what the medicine is showing you.

On many occasions, I've seen participants get so caught up in what's happening with someone else, they lose track of their own experience. The facilitator and ceremony guardians are responsible for what's going on in the room. Nine times out of ten, they're aware of any disturbances happening, so if something's bothering you, chances are they either already know about it and are watching the situation, or have their reasons for letting it be, in which case it may be your own internal distractions you need to deal with.

When empaths and healers come to ceremony, they can get caught up in what others are experiencing because they can feel it and want to help. This is an ego distraction. Unless you're a ceremony guardian, you're not responsible for taking care of anyone else but yourself in ceremony. Thinking you need to come out of your own visionary experience and save someone else is a good way to avoid looking at your own issues, so avoid the savior complex, buckle down, remain present and face your own shadows and light. If you honestly feel like someone is in danger, then of course, alert the guardian staff. Otherwise, come back to your center, stay in alignment and focus on your own prayers and intentions, not what's happening with someone else. I'll discuss ceremony protocol in more depth in Chapter 7: Before & During Ceremony – Practical Tips.

Ceremonial Hive Mind

One of the most fascinating concepts coming out of sacred medicine ceremonies is what I call the "ceremonial hive mind." All individuals present at a specific sacred medicine ceremony are at the same location on the space-time continuum, because they're supposed to be there.

Having been a guardian, I've seen up close how much flux and flow happens when planning ceremonies. People change their minds last minute, hit too much traffic and have to turn back, have strange accidents, personal emergencies or any number of complications that keep them from coming. At the same time, others who were on a waiting list, reached out at the last minute or even accidently show up on the wrong night, become a part of that night's experience.

What unfolds is always a concoction of magical components shaken together to get all the chosen people together in the right place at the right time. Invariably, at talk circle the next morning, when everyone shares their experience from the night before, there are synchronicities, unexplained patterns and themes that flow through the entire group.

It's one thing if you have an unusual vision and experience, and it's easy to talk yourself out of a paranormal event. It's another thing entirely if several other people in the circle have a similar experience. It's like a magnificent cosmic jigsaw puzzle that gets pieced together when people share their experiences in talk circle after the ceremony. No amount of conscious mind planning could account for the magic I've seen with how connected people are in ceremony. Much of the lasting healing that people receive comes from what they learn in talk circle.

When you experience ceremonial hive mind, it also helps to solidify the truth that we're all interconnected. How can such random people coming from different places, often different countries, with vastly different experiences end up in the same room at the same time and have experiences that are in alignment with each other? It defies scientific explanation but that's irrelevant when you live through the experience yourself.

Unfortunately, not all psychedelic medicine groups do a talk circle after ceremony. This is another reason why recording your experience in a journal is so important for your ongoing growth and evolution. If you need additional help, there are also highly competent psychedelic integration coaches who can assist you in making sense of your experiences after ceremony. Please see the Resources section for more information.

Understanding the concept of ceremonial hive mind can also assist in healing depression. When you have a direct experience that we're all interconnected, it can help you feel less lonely and isolated because it takes some weight off the personal burdens we all carry. When you combine this hive mind understanding with the inevitable heart-opening and compassion that flow from ceremony, it's clear why the sacred medicines are such a powerful healing path.

SET, SETTING & PROTECTION

Much discussion around psychedelic medicine ceremonies is about set and setting.

SET is about you: your mindset, your physical state, whether you're well rested, have an empty stomach that will receive the medicine. Set also includes one of the most important things to consider when communicating with the sacraments: your emotional state.

Obviously, if you've come to the spirit teachers to clear up an emotional issue, you may not be feeling great. Just pay attention to that and do what you can to show up to ceremony open to looking deeply within yourself and your life. You can do this by journaling ahead of time to get feelings off your chest, being very clear about your intentions in ceremony and/or consulting with the ceremony facilitator, a psychedelic integration coach, therapist, healer or other skilled practitioner.

Your physical state is important as well. Are you well rested and hydrated? Are you following the ceremony circle diet plan, including fasting beforehand? Most if not all sacred medicines work best when you take them on an empty stomach. In the circles I've participated in, the general guideline is to have your last meal of the day no later than 2:00pm for an evening ceremony. Again, ayahuasca is a demanding teacher, so there's a list of foods you should avoid before partaking in that sacrament in particular. Consult your ceremony facilitator for details.

One of the most crucial aspects of your *set* is your level of expectations. If there's one thing that's caused the most conflict, confusion and disappointment for ceremony participants, it's expectations! There's so much information available online now, that people often arrive to ceremony over-educated, with all kinds of stories swilling around in their heads. They're full of fear and worry and bring expectations to ceremony that have nothing at all to do with them and their personal set. If doing research ahead of time is important to you, then go for it. The Divine Mother wants you to know that no matter how much information you have prepared, it's best to let it all go, get out of your mind and surrender to the sacrament as it shows up for you in the moment.

Additionally, have you consulted with the facilitator about any medications you're taking? Some medications are contraindicated with psychedelic medicines, especially ayahuasca. For your own safety, be honest about your medications and follow your ceremony guidelines as closely as possible.

I was in ceremony once with a man who neglected to tell the facilitator that he was on a strong dose of Adderall, a central nervous system stimulant that increases dopamine and norepinephrine levels in the brain. During ceremony his blood pressure became so wildly elevated that he almost had to be carried off in an ambulance. Fortunately, the facilitator was an experienced doctor and healer and was able to stabilize the man, but that night could have ended tragically.

It may seem like a burden to follow guidelines and prepare to receive the sacraments, but the guidelines must be taken seriously. If you're not prepared to be honest about your ceremony preparation and any medication you're taking, then sacred medicine ceremony isn't the place for you at this time.

SETTING is about the environment you're in. I don't recommend using the sacraments alone until you have extensive experience in a safe group setting. Group settings usually (and should) include guardians and facilitators who can help and guide you if you're going through a rough passage. Also, group facilitators should be skilled at creating a safe setting, which includes a clean room, close proximity to bathrooms, climate regulation, no obstacles that can be tripped over during ceremony, and any other arrangements that can be made to ensure participants are comfortable.

PROTECTION is an energetic insurance policy. When you're partaking in the sacred medicines, you're entering an altered state of consciousness where your mind is massively open and expanded to allow interdimensional messages to come through. This is a vulnerable state, which is why skilled facilitators call in their own spirit guides and the spirit guides from their lineage, to energetically protect the ceremonial space and all the participants. When you leave the 3-D plane all kinds of otherworldly phenomena happen, much of it subjective, so knowing that you're energetically and psychically protected is paramount.

On top of the protection that's set up by your ceremony facilitator, I recommend you create your own energetic shield in ceremony, for your own personal space. For example, call on your guardian angels, ancestors and other spirit guides to keep you safe during ceremony. If you don't have experience with spirit guides, you can imagine yourself safe inside of an energetic bubble that's protected by your Higher Power. Anything you can do to protect yourself personally on top of the circle protection created by your facilitator is only a good thing. Pro Tip: When you ask for non-physical assistance, always remember to affirm that any assistance comes from karma-free beings of light, so you don't accidentally open yourself up to entities with their own agenda.

In the Resources section, you'll find a free shielding technique, which you can also download from my website, www.inthedivine.com

Entities

Let's have a lil' chat about what are colloquially called "entities" in the psychedelic medicine world. Entities are both disembodied beings that one sees through visions, and energetic organisms that can move from one person to the next in medicine ceremonies. When you purge in ayahuasca ceremonies, you can release entities trapped inside of your energetic body. This is a good thing because often what's ailing us is a negative energetic complex that's trapped inside of our Human Energy System.

This energetic complex can be attached to ancestral trauma, a specific traumatic event or something else in our life experience that's keeping us from growing, evolving and feeling happiness. Entities usually have an ego, drive or objective. They're similar to a parasite that feeds off of its host without killing it. Entities can be small and weak and simply dissolve into the light once they're released, or they can be large and powerful and challenging to remove and eliminate.

The worst entity I've encountered was a large being attached to an active drug addict. This man was a powerful curandero, guardian and singer/musician with years of experience working with the medicines and he was well-loved and held in high esteem in the medicine community. He had been a heroin addict years prior and unfortunately, had relapsed. Because he had been such an important part of the medicine circle for so long, the main facilitator allowed him to stay on in ceremonies, in the hopes that he'd be cured of his drug addiction.

Sadly, that meant he was allowed to assist in healing the other ceremony participants. I didn't agree with this decision and was watching the addict closely. During the ceremony he was obviously high, and not just on ayahuasca. At some point in the night, he left the circle to take a street drug and then came back in and thought he would just go back to business as usual. He was nodding off and unable to sit up straight and that's when I knew I had to take matters into my own hands.

In this circle, about two-thirds of the way into the ceremony, we brought out a healing mat so anyone who desired a hands-on healing, could receive it at the capable hands of some of the experienced ceremony guardians. Mind you, in medicine circles, talking is kept to an absolute minimum and only done in whispers, so as not to take anyone out of their visions and experience. When I saw how high the addict was, I couldn't exactly yell at him and tell him to get the hell out of there, as badly as I wanted to. Instead, I sat next to the woman on the healing mat and held her hand while I quietly planned my next move.

As I watched the addict, a big entity inside of him turned to gaze at me. It looked like an exact replica of the addict, only in ethereal, energetic form. Its face was gaunt and hollow-eyed, and it telepathically "said" to me, "I'm in charge here and I've taken over this man's body. I'm going to drain it of life as slowly as I feel like. I'm going to do whatever the hell I want and there's not a damn thing you can do about it."

That's when I got up and told the addict he needed to leave the healing mat and go back to his place in the circle. I had to be quiet, yet forceful about it, so as not to disturb the participants. Thankfully the addict complied without too much effort, but later when we were outside of the ceremony room, he got in my face and yelled at me for telling him to leave the healing mat. I was frightened, but I knew it was the demonic entity inside of him driving his actions.

Being confronted by this powerful entity was disturbing, but this is the kind of thing that can happen with the sacraments. It also showed me how substance abuse can open the door for these kinds of demonic energy complexes to take over someone's consciousness and drive them to act and live in ways that slowly kill them.

This is why I say, even if you one-hundred-percent trust the safety of the medicine circle you sit in, it still pays to shield yourself energetically and be aware of your surroundings. If something feels "off" to you, check in with the facilitator or one of the guardians to discuss it before ceremony starts. When everyone is under the influence of the medicine isn't the best time to do it.

QUALITIES OF EXPERIENCE

When it comes to ayahuasca at least, it's usually recommended that you sit in more than one ceremony in a row, usually over a Friday and Saturday night, unless you're on a longer retreat at a healing center where you may sit multiple nights in a row. I've lost count of the times that someone had planned to stay for two nights and then had what they felt was a "bad" experience on the first night and decided not to stay for the second.

How the Medicines Work

The guardian staff would always do our best to convince them to stay because we knew the truth: healing and enlightenment happen in layers. Even when you have a clear intention, you often need to scrape off an entire layer of gunk before the true healing can begin. This is why the first night can be a struggle, but what seemed hard from the night before is much more easily resolved on the second night. You can't get to the deeper level until you dig through the top layer, which can be uncomfortable.

Sadly, some people insist on leaving when they're in a shattered state, refuse the wisdom and stop the process before their best healing happens. This helps no one. The Divine Mother would like you to know that there are cycles that happen with the sacraments. One cycle begins with setting your intention for ceremony and it completes when you take action after the fact on the healings and blessings you receive in ceremony. If you leave too soon, you miss the complete healing cycle available to you.

She also wants you to know that the reverse is true. When you ingest sacred medicines, you may feel something that's best described as "absolutely nothing." The feeling that "nothing happened" can be particularly frustrating when you do a bunch of research and plan ahead, stick to the prescribed pre-ceremony diet and do all the "right things" to be prepared for ceremony. Even when you *feel* like nothing happened, the psychedelic medicine is still inside of your body, working its magic on a subtle, cellular level, so don't get discouraged if your experience is lighter that you "expected."

Ceremonies of Sacred Life

You can come to ayahuasca or other sacraments and have a gentle, loving and even erotic experience, but it won't be like that every time and you're not special and more evolved if you happen to have some easy experiences at first. It may be that you simply haven't taken a large enough dose. And it may also be that you're being slowly coaxed into deeper levels of healing. Take nothing for granted.

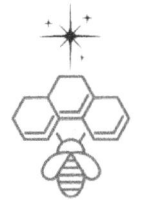

CHAPTER 4: THE GREAT KARMIC BALANCE

One of the greatest teachings from the sacraments is the concept of karma. Karma is a Sanskrit word that roughly translates to "action" and it's a core concept in some Eastern religions, including Hinduism and Buddhism. Karma relates to cause and effect — each action you take will eventually be reflected back to you. This rule also applies to your thoughts, words and the actions other people take based on your instructions. When it comes to karma, like causes produce like effects; that is, a good deed will lead to a future good effect, while a bad deed will lead to a future negative or harmful effect. Another way to think of it is "what goes around comes around."

The medicine will often show you a vast matrix of karma created by your family of origin and ancestral lineages as well as your own personal decisions. Often the heavy generational effects of war, genocide, slavery and other traumas are unconsciously passed down through generations, even when people leave the regions where the atrocities took place. That means they're walking around day-to-day with not only their own personal life challenges, but also a heavy dose of ancestral karma, which can weigh their spirits down.

I've seen time and again that participants from war-torn regions of the world, or countries with a long history of conflict, genocide, slavery and other upheavals may have unconscious layers of darkness that release during a sacred ceremony - ayahuasca in particular. Since ayahuasca dismantles the psyche and clears out destructive complexes to cleanse consciousness, these issues ooze out in ceremony and can be released through purging. When the medicine releases your ancestral karma, it instigates healing both backwards into the past and forward into the future. How does that work? Again, no one knows *exactly*, but on multiple occasions, I've had a visceral experience of releasing ancestral karma.

One of my ayahuasca mentors used to say, "After you purge, contemplate your bucket." In other words, look into your purge bucket so you know precisely what issues you've just released. You're probably thinking, "Gross - no way do I want to look at it!" but I've had some profound experiences doing just that.

In one ceremony, I purged from my stomach into my bucket and when I gazed inside, a gathering of my ancestors gazed back and lovingly thanked me for setting them free. I come from a long line of oppressed indigenous peoples from North America, so experiencing their liberation was deeply emotional for me and I felt immense lightness afterwards. This lightness allowed me to let go of some negative behaviors and it changed my life going forward. In this instance, ayahuasca helped me release heavy karma that my ancestors carried, *and* it helped me release the karmic burden of the fear, anxiety, anger and bad decisions I was making in my present, daily life. This is the power of ayahuasca and other sacred medicines – to create profound healing all along the space-time continuum.

As I mentioned previously, many sacred medicines activate the natural DMT and other receptors already present in your brain and body and dismantle the conscious mind rigidity that's required for you to operate in the 3-D world. The mind takes in massive quantities of information every single moment and according to the philosophies of Neuro-Linguistic Programming (NLP), the only way we can function in a sane way is when the brain deletes, distorts and generalizes some information, essentially subduing any information not needed in the moment. We're not wired to operate consciously with the full load of information our brain is constantly absorbing – it would be too overwhelming for our nervous systems.

Integrating these vast, interconnected insights usually requires you to take action in your waking life on the lessons you learned in ceremony. If you skip that homework because it feels uncomfortable and then come right back to ceremony to relieve your discomfort, you're missing the point. The Divine Mother reminds you that the sacraments are here to help humanity evolve, not to keep us spinning around in our emotional blocks without getting past them.

When you sit with the sacraments over time, the otherworldly visions, ideas, feelings and connections you receive in sacred ceremony, make more sense in your day-to-day life as you become aware of the interconnectedness of life. You start to ask deeper questions about yourself, your life, how we're all related to each other in one way or another and how we're all operating out of past experiences as well as future desires. The Divine Mother wants you to understand that this unfolding awareness is *the* pathway to compassion, and compassion is the pathway to human evolution.

She also wants you to know that this new awareness is the seed of light that grows into your ability to expand and trust your intuition. Intuition is a base-level skill that the psychedelic medicines awaken in you to uplift your humanity into enlightenment. She is adamant that you understand this and accept that the ONLY thing preventing you from using your intuition to set yourself free is your own SELF-DOUBT. Nothing else stands in the way.

INTUITION & FREE WILL

"If the doors of perception were cleansed, every thing would appear to man as it is: infinite." – Quote attributed to the poet William Blake, (1757 – 1827)

You are a creator and manifestor of all that you desire, including health, wealth, love and happiness. The sacred teachers are here to pave the way for you, but you must get out of your own way and the easiest way to do that is to eliminate self-doubt.

Intuition is the ability to understand and "know" something immediately, without the need for conscious, rational reasoning. We're all born with intuition – it's our birthright. The reason I became a teacher of intuition is because I've been highly intuitive since I was a young child. I had my first psychic experience at the age of nine, when I "heard" my great-grandmother talking to me. Because this gift has been part of my life since forever, I didn't realize everyone didn't have the same thing until I was in my 30s. The more I talked about psychic abilities and intuition, the clearer it was that everyone else had experienced it to some degree, they just didn't understand or know how to use it.

I've learned that most people tend to have similar doubts and misgivings about their own intuition. They ask the same questions: "Is it real?" and "How do I know I can trust it?" These misgivings come from self-doubt, which is understandable, since intuition is trained right out of us from the time we're little. Schools, religions and most families have no support structure to foster the ongoing growth and development of intuitive abilities.

This is where the spirit teachers come in. They show you what's on the other side of the rigid, 3-D conscious mind structure we all live by. They show you the alternate dimensions that have an influence on your behaviors and the pathway to use that knowledge to improve your life and the lives of those around you. The trick is to act on that information, and the only thing stopping you is your level of self-doubt.

Your thoughts create your reality, so if your thoughts are that it's right, normal and possible for you to build and trust your intuition, that's what you'll do. But when you doubt yourself, that's also a thought. Self-doubt slows down your enlightenment because it's as subtle as intuition and it will run your life if you remain unaware of it.

The longer you sit in ceremony with the sacraments, the better chances you have of increasing your intuition and psychic abilities. Psychic abilities are just heightened experiences of communicating via alternate dimensions. In other words, psychic abilities allow you to experience things outside the physical realm as we know it and the sacred medicines are your tour guides for these experiences.

Psychedelic visions often usher in claircognizance, which is the ability to acquire knowledge without knowing how or why you know it. You just KNOW. When our DMT receptors are activated, adding to the other intracellular activity that happens while on the sacred medicine, the rigidity of mind you rely on to operate normally, is removed. Your mind is vastly expanded from its usual 3-D state, and you have awareness of the trans-dimensional reality beyond the 3-D world. The *awareness* is the key, and it awakens when your doors of perception are opened by the spirit teachers. How you deal with that information is based on your set, setting, protection and intentions, as well as your willingness to believe in the power of your intuition.

The Divine Mother wants you to know that intuition represents your connection with source consciousness, or God. When you access and use your intuition, you're using a hotline to God. When you use your intuition along with your conscious mind, plus the knowledge you've gained from accessing alternate dimensions, you're a human being who's one-hundred-percent independent and free from manipulation by others.

She wants you to know that at this time in history, it's crucial for people to use their intuition because of all the darkness, fearmongering and manipulation that's playing out on the world stage around the pandemic-fear-event and what's to come afterward. A population in fear is easy to control, which is why dark forces focus very diligently to pump a constant stream of fear through all media outlets. When you're in fear, it's much harder to access your intuition properly, which puts you at a deep disadvantage to protect yourself and find the light of truth, which comes directly from source consciousness.

When you communicate with the sacred medicines, take heed of the lessons you learn from them, record them in your journal, and diligently make changes in your life based on what you've learned. Very soon you'll sense that you're a sovereign being, fully independent and free from manipulation. Think about that for a moment...

Imagine if everyone stopped what they were doing and decided to trust their intuition. Would we have anarchy, or would we have peace? If we had a new zeitgeist where people trusted the innate healing power of their own bodies and were able to make the best health decisions for themselves and their families, how would that have changed history?

Of course, there's no way to answer that question, but it's clear that the current political climate is spewing force and submission with the powerful weapon of fear. The sacraments don't preach fear. Their message is love, compassion, acceptance and freedom. Could this be why most entheogens are illegal in many countries? Wouldn't a population that had unlimited access to messages directly from God and the ability to act on those messages, be impossible to control and coerce through fear?

If you represented a ruling entity responsible for moving a population in the direction you wanted, when and how you wanted, wouldn't a consciousness-expanding substance that increased intuition and liberated minds out of fearful living be public enemy number one? The Divine Mother asks you to consider these questions and see where that questioning takes you.

She also reminds you that you live on a free-will planet. She won't tell you specifically what to do. That's up to you. She asks you to consider whether domination and fearmongering is in support of compassion, awareness, presence and oneness, which are what the psychedelic medicines teach. You must make decisions on your own and act on them according to your free will. She is only pointing the way for you. Humanity must rise up and become enlightened on its own and trusting and building intuition is a simple first step. The sacred teachers create a space where you may question whether your current will is serving your best interests or whether it's serving the interests of those who want to keep you fearful and compliant.

For an easy process to learn how to use your intuition, see the Resources section.

Growth & Expansion

In order to elevate humanity and strengthen free will, the psychedelic medicines are expanding their exposure as the world becomes more imbalanced. This is why cannabis and psilocybin are being decriminalized in more places and ayahuasca is a more common topic of conversation across the globe than ever before.

The Divine Mother wants you to know that the sacraments are hearing the call of humanity. Since they enlighten humanity toward compassion, the need for more compassion creates a greater need for the medicine, so it's expanding outward to every country on the planet to fulfill this need. The pilgrimage outward is not an easy one for the medicines because human ego is involved. In other words, things are getting messy! Hence the Divine Mother's need for the messages within this book to be communicated across the globe.

With an increase in demand for the sacraments and ceremonial work, comes a push for more supply and that's how the delicate balance held for sacred medicine work becomes disrupted. In the late 1950s, the author R. Gordon Wasson met with Maria Sabina, a curandera from the Mazatec culture, who lived deep in the mountains of Oaxaca, Mexico. She came from a curandero lineage and was skilled in the ways of the *veleda*, or ancient Mazatec psilocybin healing ceremony. Wasson initially kept her information private per her request, but eventually published her name and location in some of his writings.

Soon people from all over the world descended upon her rural community and during the 1960s counterculture revolution, people started taking mushrooms to "get high." As the indigenous reverence for the sacred mushroom that had been woven into life was abandoned by the outsiders, the local community was thrown into turmoil. Maria was ostracized and her home was burned down. The attention from the outside was ultimately tragic for the local community, culture and for Maria herself as her son was murdered during the upheaval.

A similar story is unfolding today as ayahuasca ritual tourism increases and expands throughout the Amazon, Costa Rica and beyond, deep into the jungles and indigenous communities. In 2018, 81-year-old Olivia Arèvalo Lomas, a highly revered curandera, defender of the Peruvian Amazon and elder in the Peruvian Shipibo-konibo community in Yarinacocha, Peru, was shot in the chest and murdered outside her home, by a Caucasian Canadian man, Sebastian Woodroffe. He was later dragged through the streets, lynched and killed by indigenous members of the local community.

Allegedly, Woodroffe had been taking anti-psychotic and other pharmaceutical drugs, potentially at the same time he was drinking ayahuasca. He was known both in Canada and in the local Yarinacocha community to be mentally unstable and clearly shouldn't have been drinking ayahuasca, especially at the same time as taking these types of pharmaceutical drugs. It's vitally important to pay attention to diet and medical guidelines for sacred medicine, ayahuasca in particular, but no one can police someone's actions 24/7 and honoring the indigenous traditions settles mostly in the heart. You must take responsibility for your own integrity and health. Clearly, even with the best of intentions, Western lifestyle and mindset often leave a destructive residue as they weave through indigenous cultures.

As more people come to the psychedelic medicines, the Divine Mother is concerned that they're not properly equipped for the adventure. Many are becoming lost in the interdimensional exploration and are distracted by the outer trappings and image of being a medicine ceremony participant, but not doing the deep inner work that goes hand-in-hand with an expanded consciousness.

Ayahuasca and other sacraments aren't a cure-all for your life issues because they cannot fix everything that ails you. They can only guide you into the light and into compassion and awareness. They do this in part by creating the space for your intuition to increase. The rest is up to you. As I've mentioned previously, it's tempting to relieve your life discomfort with a revolving door into another ceremony. When this continues to happen, it's easy to grasp onto the ongoing mystical adventure and become detached from your daily life.

The Divine Mother wants to be clear that while it's vital to spread Her message far and wide, losing yourself in the medicine isn't the answer. It's destructive to your personal growth, overall health and relationships because being in the 5-D interdimensional realm will take a toll on you if you don't ground yourself into your earth-bound reality. You must tend to your business, your finances, your health and your family first. She cannot do it for you. She can guide you to the knowledge you need to keep your life balanced, but the balancing you must do yourself. Don't fool yourself by thinking you don't have to be compliant with gravity. You live on this planet. Stay tethered to it while you do your inner work.

1ST CHAKRA ISSUES

According to ancient Eastern philosophy, the body has chakras, or wheels of energy that spin in specific locations of the body. The word "chakra" is the Sanskrit word for wheel. Here in the West, many people think of these wheels as two-dimensional energy centers located down the spinal column because that's how they're depicted in print. But the more expanded definition is that they're third-dimensional vortices of energy, extending in all directions, in multiple planes and corresponding to specific organ systems and specific life issues. In other words, chakras affect your mental, physical and spiritual aspects. In order to function as a holistic Human Energy System, it's beneficial to take all chakras into account. You could read entire books on the chakras, and if you wanted to have a deeper understanding of the Human Energy System, simply studying the chakras would be enough.

Here's a brief overview of the seven chakras to support how the sacred medicines can influence and guide you:

The 1st/root chakra is associated with issues of security, safety, food, shelter and livelihood and corresponds to the perineum/anus and organs of elimination.

The 2nd/sacral chakra is associated with creativity, sexuality and relationship with others and corresponds to the sexual/reproductive organs.

The 3rd/solar-plexus chakra is associated with issues of power and corresponds to the stomach and digestive organs.

The 4th/heart chakra is associated with love and corresponds to the heart and circulatory systems.

The 5th/throat chakra is associated with communication and corresponds to the thyroid gland in the neck.

The 6th/third-eye chakra is associated with intuition and corresponds to the pineal gland, in the area between the eyes. The pineal gland produces and excretes the hormone melatonin, responsible for managing sleep cycles.

The 7th/crown chakra is associated with spiritual consciousness and enlightenment. It sits at the top of the head and corresponds to the pituitary gland, which secretes the hormones that maintain homeostasis in the body.

Many people come to the sacraments as a last resort and they're in such a bad place, they don't possess the funds to pay their facilitator. This is normally handled on a case-by-case basis, but if you constantly show up to the medicine seeking a handout, perhaps it's time to ask yourself if you have the correct approach. Most facilitators run ceremonies because they're called from their hearts to do so. Training to run medicine circles can take years and many facilitators spend significant cash completing their training.

Preparing each ceremony also requires time and financial resources. The logistics of a single ceremony alone can be mind-boggling. Most facilitators are open to a few work-trade spots or discounts for some ceremony participants, but facilitators deserve to be paid for their services. If you regularly show up to the medicine in a state of desperation because you don't have the resources to organize your life and finances, perhaps coming to ceremony isn't where you should be placing your focus and energy. The sacred medicines can't balance your finances for you or help you generate the income required to live the life you desire, a life which includes coming to sacred ceremony.

The Divine Mother wants you to know that when you repeatedly come to ceremony while you're having 1st chakra/survival issues and nothing ever changes, it's time to take a good, hard look at your approach for ensuring your own ability to thrive on the physical plane. Don't use the sacraments to feel better about your life without putting in the work required to change your life so you can get past the issues that constantly keep you at a survival level.

1st chakra issues are a slippery slope to manipulating and being manipulated by sexual energy as well. Much of this happens unconsciously and is magnified by the intensity of the medicine. The 1st chakra rules all, which means that if you're operating from unconscious fears and insecurities about your basic needs being met, they will drive your behaviors and choices - there's no way around it. That unconscious desperation can be expressed through sexual energy, which is heightened by the effects of the medicine.

If you legitimately need help once or twice to get to ceremony, of course, ask for it. But if you find yourself always needing a handout or a discount in order to sit with the medicine and you're offering little in return, perhaps it's time to take a break from ceremony and get your 3-D life in order. It feels wonderful to have your heart and crown chakras activated by the medicines, but if your life is stuck at 1st chakra level, the fear that comes along with it will shut down the work your 4th /heart chakra and 7th/crown chakra are wanting to do. Until you master your 1st chakra survival issues, your life will remain in a diminished state.

Obviously, it's not easy to pull yourself out of poverty and everyone deserves to experience the sacraments. Just be aware of how much you're taking and asking for vs. what you're giving in return. Also be aware of how much focus you're putting into coming to ceremony vs. how much focus you're putting into pulling yourself out of 1st chakra desperation and be mindful of keeping an ethical balance.

BATHE YOUR MIND BEFORE CEREMONY

The Divine Mother wishes you to know that She's deeply concerned about spiritual casualties - the people who receive the sacraments and then think they're spiritually evolved but are not. The reason, once again, is because they're caught up in the medicine experience and aren't doing their healing and integration work outside of ceremony to support the vibrational changes happening inside of them. People at this level tend to spiritually bypass by using a cloak of spirituality to deflect wrongdoing or deeper unhealed emotions in themselves and others, rather than confronting the issues directly.

When you communicate with the sacraments, your vibration changes, your perspective changes – you're just different overall. Because these vibrational changes are so profound, it's easy to stop there and think your work is complete when you leave ceremony and snuggle up to those yummy, open-hearted feelings. Because the sacred medicines are increasing their exposure, there are more incidences of people getting stuck at this level. When you're surrounded by a community that loves being together in ceremony, it's tempting to keep going back for the experience, rather than spending time going within and doing the inner shifting that's truly required to permanently raise your vibration and be of service to planetary oneness.

The Divine Mother asks that before you go on a psychedelic journey, consider where you are emotionally and ask yourself if you're truly ready for interdimensional travel at this time. Have you done the homework assigned to you from your last experience? Are you making the necessary changes in your life to keep rising up in vibrational alignment? Are you going to back to ceremony because you feel uncomfortable in your life? What efforts have you actually made to change your current situation?

If you're not making an effort to change your life, then you're probably in the middle of a spiritual bypass and ripe for projecting that energy onto others instead of healing and dealing with it within yourself. In this case, going back to ceremony is a greedy waste of the sacraments. The Divine Mother would like you to know that the spirit teachers are here to guide you, but no teacher likes a student who's not paying attention in class and then repeatedly asks the same questions that have already been answered.

If you want to be a masterful student of the sacred teachers, then honor their wisdom. Reflect on it. Process it. Integrate it. Really feel it in your bones before you go back for another experience. Continuously returning to ceremony without doing your homework is like going back for a second or third plate at dinner without paying attention to your hunger levels. It's wasteful and potentially harmful to you.

In the Resources section, I've shared some journaling prompts for ceremony. Using the journaling system I've developed helps you keep track of your progress and evaluate whether you're truly ready to go back to ceremony, or if you're just avoiding the work required to solve your problems.

Communing with the sacred medicines, fasting, adjusting your diet ahead of time, traveling to get there and back and being off your usual sleep routine, all take a toll on the Human Energy System. Coming back from ceremony and re-integrating into your life takes effort as well. Skipping the integration step could very well be the cause of the feeling that you need to turn right around and come back into ceremony, so give yourself plenty of time to rest and reflect before you fully return to your life after ceremony.

PERILS & PITFALLS OF CEREMONY CIRCLES

When I first started coming to ayahuasca circles in 2012, they seemed so mysterious, complex and dramatic. I encountered a new type of people, ritual and knowledge and it all felt so *important* and far outside my comfort zone. At that time, I'd been studying spirituality, personal growth and human potential for over twenty-five years. I thought I'd seen it all, but this world was *different* - strange and unusual in so many ways. For the first few ceremonies I felt stupid and humbled by something that happened right before or right after I left, yet I kept coming back because I sensed it was the next step in my growth, evolution, enlightenment and service to the greater good.

I didn't have a lot of extra cash when I first started out, so there were long blocks of time between ceremonies for me. I used that time to continue working on my spiritual and personal evolution, which has been part of my daily life for decades. I slowly moved into the inner realm of my medicine circle and for a long time, I felt like I'd finally arrived at the place I was meant to be, surrounded by my true and real tribe. Then the blinders got lifted off my eyes and I saw a dark truth that I now know exists inside of every medicine circle: despite our best efforts, we humans tend to

The Great Karmic Balance

make a mess of things everywhere we go, and the sacraments magnify human frailties.

I thought the senior people in the circle were truly evolved and had access to some higher level of celestial magic dust that would somehow be sprinkled upon me the higher up I went in the circle, the more ayahuasca I drank and the more I made myself available in service to others. And... the time for my celestial magic dust benediction never came because it doesn't exist.

The situation with the drug addict that I mentioned in Chapter 3: How the Medicines Work, was the final event in a list of inconsistent and unethical actions inside my circle. As a guardian and healer, I had a karmic responsibility to protect the woman on the healing mat. Her consciousness was open, she was surrendered to healing and a demonic entity was attempting to connect with her exposed and vulnerable consciousness. That is a karmic violation of the highest order, and I wasn't going to be any part of it. Because I no longer felt like this circle was safe and in integrity, I left later that night, and it was a couple of years before I returned. Even though the addict was finally gone by then, the circle was never the same for me because I was concerned that the ceremonial space wasn't properly protected.

Most facilitators sacrifice a lot to do what they do. Many of them have dealt with near death experiences and illnesses and various and assorted traumas. Because of that, they're called to commit their lives to doing the deep service of holding circle for others. They still need to be paid and support themselves as well.

These souls are usually skilled and experienced and many of them are trained in different disciplines and medicine lineages. But every facilitator, ayahuasero/a, shaman and curandero/a is still a fallible, finite human being. Many of them have ongoing addiction issues themselves. They aren't ascended masters, bodhisattvas or karma-free, angelic beings of light. They're still subject to ego, bad decisions, mistakes and greed. None of them are perfect and neither are you.

In full disclosure, I was accused of being harsh and too direct in my communication, which is the type of energetic vibration that can be magnified while under the influence of the sacraments. I accept that critical feedback and have remained aware of it and continue to work on it. I'm far from perfect and I acknowledge that I have strong energy and can be too much for some people if I don't stay mindful of communicating in a gentle way, especially while under the influence of the sacred medicines.

When the big drug addict entity revealed himself to me, I was focused on getting him out of there as quickly as possible and wasn't considering the tone I used. Long after I left the circle, I learned there had been gossip, accusations and assumptions, and the tone I used with the addict became the main issue, not that he was at the healing mat in the first place.

It was a simple problem that could have been cleared up at a guardian meeting before or after ceremony, which is part of the management of many medicine circles. Since our circle didn't hold staff meetings, the issue was allowed to smolder, and no one came to me directly with their concerns about my communication. I now understand that without direct, heartfelt, regular, open communication among the staff, there's no way to prevent internal problems from festering and spreading.

It's true that this kind of thing can happen in any personal or professional group – it's not isolated to the sacred medicine. What's also true is that every organization reflects its leadership. Whatever flaws a leader has, gets trickled all the way down throughout the organization. This is particularly problematic in medicine circles, because the Divine Mother is pushing for growth at a vibrational, cellular level, which heightens core wounds and emotions. Whatever lessons the group needs to learn are forced through by the sacraments, so if the leadership isn't resolving its flaws, then the flaws trickle down to the guardians, the quality of the ceremony and to the ceremony participants themselves.

It was the leadership energy that allowed a functioning addict to participate on the healing mat and put participants in psychic danger. It was that same leadership energy that allowed internal misunderstandings to fester within the guardian staff, never get resolved and then ultimately set the stage for the senior guardian women (not just me), to leave the circle over time. If the circle leader has substance abuse issues, they'll show up in the circle. If the leader has problems with strong feminine energy, that will be a problem within the circle as well. I could give you a hundred different examples, but you get the point. In sacred medicine circles, there's nowhere to hide. Everything gets revealed under the unyielding gaze of the Divine Mother.

I felt heartbroken and utterly *shattered* about what happened in my main medicine circle, especially because I was excluded from ceremony when things picked up again during the pandemic-fear-event in 2020. This was a deeply lonely and sad time when the world was in isolation, and we all needed the sacraments more than ever. It was an opportunity for my medicine family to come together in oneness to heal the circle issues and start anew, but instead they chose to give in to gossip and avoid real communication. It took some time before I got past the hurt and began to heal around what had happened.

It helped when I spoke to a medicine brother who's been drinking ayahuasca and working with sacred medicines for over 30 years. He told me he's been in 13 medicine circles and run a few of his own over the years and the same thing happens in each and every circle – they eventually get blown apart by some type of human drama.

The Divine Mother wants you to know She's not weaving a cloak of instability and deception for us wee little humans to deal with. She simply continues to flow Her energy towards enlightenment and compassion and it's our inability to shift that creates conflict, hurt and misunderstandings within psychedelic medicine circles. So when you're thinking it's easier and more fun to come back to ceremony instead of integrating and healing your issues, think again. It's true that magic is created when the sacred medicine is flowing and you're touching the mind and hands of God, but that doesn't absolve you of your humanity. Partaking of the sacrament doesn't magically keep anyone from behaving like an asshole (myself included). Remember that and keep doing your inner and outer work.

CHAPTER 5: THE CELESTIAL INFORMATION SUPERHIGHWAY

The Divine Mother is always available to communicate with you and the sacred medicines are vehicles for this interdimensional communication. However, She feels that many at this time in history aren't listening because they just come to Her for the "high."

When you come to ceremony without being grounded, it's easy to get caught up in the experience, but experiences are available everywhere. Why specifically do you want to come to ceremony and what do you expect to see when you get there? Are you here to stand for the earth, for all people, for love? Are you here to gain a deeper understanding of life? For what purpose? What will you do with that deeper understanding? Will you keep it in your pocket, or will you share it with others? Are you coming to ceremony to make new friends and new connections? What will you do with those connections? When you ask these questions of your psychedelic medicine work, your answers will ground you deeper in your purpose and help you understand how you can best utilize the sacraments going forward.

Our Celestial Family

In ayahuasca ceremonies there are various entity "themes" that show up for many people. It's often animals, jaguars, snakes, some type of spaceship or machine and there are also alien beings. While it's easy to see and experience these Celestial Beings while sitting with ayahuasca, with intention and experience, you can experience them in meditation and also via cannabis and other sacraments.

THE ENDOCANNABINOID SYSTEM

The Divine Mother would like you to know that the Celestial Beings brought cannabis to the planet millennia ago to be used as a vehicle to communicate with them. One of the reasons this communication is possible is because of the endocannabinoids within the Human Energy System. I've been instructed not to go too deeply into science here because the Divine Mother wants the main focus of this book to be her channeled messages. There are plenty of articles and books that detail the science of the endocannabinoid system and psychedelic medicines. If you desire information about Western scientific research and experiments, a simple online search will return many science-based options for you.

For a brief overview, there are compounds in cannabis plants called cannabinoids, and there are also endogenous (organically made inside the body) cannabinoids called endocannabinoids. The endocannabinoid system exists throughout the body's nervous system. Currently, there are also two known cannabinoid receptors in the body that bind to endocannabinoids for the purpose of signaling that the endocannabinoid system needs to take some type of action. To date, science isn't exactly sure of the purpose of this system, but it's believed the endocannabinoid system helps the body maintain homeostasis (continuous internal balance), beginning at the cellular level.

While there may be over 100 cannabinoids in the sacrament of cannabis, three are commonly known: tetrahydrocannabinoid or THC, which is the primary psychoactive (affecting the mind) compound in cannabis. This is the compound that gives you a "high" feeling when smoking or ingesting cannabis. Once it's in your system, it binds to both of your cannabinoid receptors. This allows THC to have a powerful effect on your body and mind.

Cannabidiol (CBD) is non-psychoactive, and cannabinol (CBN) is moderately psychoactive and present in higher concentrations when cannabis has been aged and stored. There's usually very little CBN in fresh plants and it's believed that CBD doesn't interact with the endocannabinoid receptors in the same way as THC does. Current science still has more to learn about the specifics of how these compounds work and it's believed that there may be more types of cannabinoids, yet undiscovered.

In the flower/bloom of the plant there are also terpenes, which are aromatic compounds that create the characteristic scent of many plants. Terpenes can attract pollinators to plants and also

The Celestial Information Superhighway

repel predators. They are bioactive (affecting the body) and are the primary constituents of essential oils. Terpenes are the basis of the science of aromatherapy, which uses essential oils for therapeutic benefit.

The Celestial Beings wanted to give humans the means to communicate, receive mentorship and assistance from their higher realms of consciousness so that humans could evolve into oneness and wholeness. Since this is a free-will planet, the Celestial Beings cannot enforce their will upon us. Cannabis then, is a *Celestial Information Superhighway* between us and them, available at any time.

Cannabis may be one of the oldest plants used by humans continuously throughout history and archaeologists have traced its use to the Neolithic Age. Based on my research, it appears that cannabis was used throughout history and across the globe, medicinally, as an aphrodisiac (a substance that arouses sexual desire), for divination (communicating with Spirit/God/source consciousness), in religious rites and was possibly also used recreationally.

The Rigveda, an ancient Indian collection of Vedic Sanskrit hymns, repeatedly sings the praises of *soma*. Many experts believe that *soma* is a drink made from cannabis, used in religious rites and divination for thousands of years. *Bhang*, which is a drink a great many scholars believe is similar to the ancient *soma*, is still made and consumed as part of religious rites in India today, in honor of

Ceremonies of Sacred Life

the god Shiva and at holy festivals. Bhang has also been used as in tantric rituals that have sexual elements to them.

The Scythians, an ancient nomadic tribal people who lived around the area of Western Siberia and all the way to the Black Sea and beyond, were well known for their cultural and religious use of cannabis, including its use in death rites. Most active from around 900 BCE (and probably earlier), the Scythians played a large role in the development of the Silk Road, and it's believed they spread cannabis to the various cultures they encountered along the way.

From the 4th century AD, many Taoist texts mention the use of cannabis that was burned in ritual censers which allowed one to breathe in its fumes. There's also evidence that cannabis was used as an aphrodisiac by the ancient Chinese. In 2003, a 2,800-year-old Caucasian-looking mummy was discovered in Turpan, Xinjiang, China. He was buried with two pounds of cannabis leaves and other funerary objects, which led archaeologists to believe that he was a shaman who probably used the sacred plant for both healing and divination.

Cannabis use in ancient Egypt was discovered in archaeological sites and in fact, Seshat, the Egyptian goddess of wisdom, knowledge and writing, is carved in the Luxor temple complex with a 7-pointed leaf over her head. Many scholars believe the leaf to be cannabis, which makes sense when you consider how working with the Celestial Information Superhighway can increase your knowledge, wisdom and creative expression.

The Celestial Information Superhighway

In 1903, an ancient Viking ship was discovered within a burial mound on a farm in Oseberg, Norway. The ship contained many grave goods and the remains of two women from a wealthy class. Scientific analysis of timbers in the grave chamber dates the burial to the autumn of 834 and among the grave goods was a small leather pouch full of cannabis seeds. It's believed that the two women could have been priestesses of Freya, the Scandinavian goddess of love, beauty, fertility, sex, war, gold, and the ability to see and influence the future. It's speculated that the cannabis seeds were used in erotic religious rites tied to priestesses of Freya, but since pagan religious beliefs were distorted with the rise of Christianity, there's no way to know why these highly revered women were buried with cannabis seeds, but clearly, the seeds were important enough to be included in the wealth of the grave goods.

In the archaeological sites that show cannabis use, it's related either to religious rites or for medicinal purposes. In some cultures, cannabis use was kept secret in the temples, and wasn't widely used by the whole population. This may be why there isn't more evidence of the exact way it was used as an aphrodisiac in sacred rites. In other cultures, like the Scythians, it appears that cannabis use was a normal part of tribal life. Of course, we'll never know every reason ancient people used cannabis, and undoubtedly it was used for recreational purposes in some cultures. However, the archaeological evidence proves time and again that the sacred plant was highly revered and used in spiritual practices and to connect with higher beings.

Ceremonies of Sacred Life

This reverent connection with cannabis has been passed down through countless generations, but during the rise of colonialism and Christianity, cannabis use was frowned upon and slowly removed from religious rites. In 1484, Pope Innocent VIII issued a papal ban on cannabis, believing it was connected to witchcraft and used in satanic masses. This is one of the reasons much of the ancient use of cannabis as an aphrodisiac and medicinal plant have been all but lost. By the 20th century it was banned in many countries, including the United States. Criminalizing this sacred plant sent it underground, almost permanently divesting it from its ancient use as a religious and erotic tool and means to connect to higher consciousness.

Cannabis is now being decriminalized slowly but surely across the United States and other countries. As use becomes more widespread, the deeper spiritual components and potential of this plant is still unknown to most. If you only use cannabis to get high, have fun, party, numb out and check out of your life (if only temporarily), you miss the loving guidance, sexual awakening and ascension that's available to you. Your body has the receptors to receive celestial guidance via cannabis, so all you need to do is approach the sacred plant in more of a reverent, prayerful, and intentional way. When you do this, as the cannabis links up with your cannabinoid receptors, it opens a portal to the Celestial Information Superhighway, allowing you to receive interdimensional guidance. Intention is key here, so when you work with cannabis, consider setting an intention to be more receptive to

The Celestial Information Superhighway

the higher wisdom available to you. This includes using cannabis in a sacred as well as an erotic way. I'll discuss this more in Chapter 6 - Cosmorgasmic Energy.

The Divine Mother would like you to know that the more closely linked you are in your heart and mind to the sacred plants you consume, the easier it'll be to consciously and unconsciously connect with the messages from the Celestial Beings. When I studied Hawai'ian spirituality in Hawai'i, I learned to always consult with any plant and ask its permission before picking or cutting it. We were taught to approach all of Hawai'i with reverence, including lava rocks, which can be easily overlooked as insignificant, but each element and part of the earth has consciousness and it's the same for cannabis.

Even if your only use for cannabis is doctor-prescribed pain or anxiety relief, it's still beneficial to approach it with reverence. Consider setting an intention for healing your condition. Modern medicine doesn't understand the Human Energy System or take it into account, so the advice you receive from doctors about medical conditions will always be limited. Cannabis (and the other sacraments) give you an opportunity to receive medical wisdom from the Celestial Beings that you wouldn't find anywhere else.

If you're asking yourself, "How do I know that I can trust information I receive from Celestial Beings?" that's a great question! In Chapter 4: The Great Karmic Balance, I discussed the importance of using your intuition. Your intuition is the vehicle through which you can understand and apply guidance from the

Celestial Beings. There are plenty of options for learning to use your intuition available online and I share an easy technique in the Resources section. However, as I said earlier, the best way to start building your intuition is to release the concept of self-doubt from your consciousness. Intuition stems from self-love and self-doubt is the opposite of self-love.

THE CANNABIS INDUSTRY

As cannabis use becomes more widespread, the global cannabis industry expands exponentially. In order to control the dosage of specific cannabis compounds, these widespread industrial complexes use chemical solvents to refine, process and filter the sacred cannabis plant. Solvents are chemicals that are mostly in liquid form and are used to dissolve, suspend or extract other materials, usually without changing the chemical structure of the materials themselves. This same process is used for personal care products, many cleaning products and pharmaceutical drugs. Some examples of solvents used on the sacred plants are butane, ethanol, propane and CO_2.

While the science makes sense, the problem is that pulling solvents through cannabis alters the sacrament until the pure spirit guardian within it may also be pulled out. Some of these products can be processed further to pull out the solvents. These products are called "solvent-free." When using cannabis products that are processed to this degree, it may be harder to "hear" or receive the Celestial Information Superhighway guidance. Be aware of that fact when considering your use of cannabis products manufactured with solvents and synthesized chemicals.

The Divine Mother would like you to understand that the edible candies and other manufactured cannabis products can be useful in some circumstances, but they are very different than extractions made more organically, with heat, pressure, oil and/or water. Cannabis has been processed organically since ancient times to create tinctures and other medicinal products. Today, products made via these methods are called "solventless."

She wants you to educate yourself about the differences in how cannabis products are created and take responsibility for the products you choose. The more processing a plant goes through, and the more chemicals added to it, the farther it is from its original form. Highly processed cannabis gummies, candies, and resins have a powerful psychoactive and physical effect, which cannot be denied. However, if you want to use processed cannabis edibles and other extracts to receive celestial guidance, also experiment with the organic plant matter and solventless products to see which form of the medicine allows you the clearest communication from the Celestial Information Superhighway.

Additionally, the cannabis industry has raked in around $20 billion dollars in 2021 alone. They're deeply invested in you buying their products. That means they spend massive marketing dollars to convince you that manufactured cannabis products, sold like candy, can make your dreams come true. Be mindful of how these companies market to you and entice you to choose new products that have little to do with the original sacrament, including the molecular structure of the whole plant. When the plant sacrament is highly processed in a lab, the solvents are used to remove components of the plants that are deemed "not necessary." But without approaching the plant sacrament in a reverent way, how does one know what is "necessary" and what isn't? It's entirely possible that the connection to the Celestial Information Superhighway is mostly removed from these manufactured products. Until you experiment, there's no way you'll know for certain if solvent-processed cannabis products will allow you a deep connection with the Celestial Beings.

Even though the cannabis industry train has long left the station, I invite you to consider if our current approach to this sacred plant is the best course for humanity. Like cannabis, the opium poppy has been in use for thousands of years. The first known recorded mention of opium is from an ancient Sumerian clay tablet, which has a list of medications of that time. Because opium is highly addictive, we turned to science to help manage this powerful sacred plant medicine. Since the early 1800s when morphine was first isolated from opium by Friedrich Wilhelm Adam Serturner, the opium poppy plant has become more of a concept than a sacred teacher as we've abandoned the plant itself for purely synthesized chemicals manufactured in a lab. But where has that gotten us?

According to the Lancet Public Health Editorial Vol. 7, Issue 3, E195, March 01, 2022:

"The opioid epidemic is one of the worst public health disasters affecting the USA and Canada. Over the past two decades, nearly 600,000 people have died from an opioid overdose in these two countries, and an estimated 1·2 million people could die from opioid overdoses by 2029."

For clarification, an opiate is a compound derived from the opium poppy. Some examples are opium, codeine and morphine. Opioids are fully synthesized, manufactured opium-based substances. There's a direct line that can be traced from that ancient Sumerian clay tablet to one of the most dangerous opioids available today: fentanyl - estimated to be 80 times as potent as morphine and hundreds of times stronger than heroin. Science chose to synthesize the opium poppy plant to make the addictive aspects of it more manageable, and in the process, created a monster of addiction that's far more destructive than the plant ever was.

The motivation behind this long journey from the 1800s to today is the same motivation that began in the Age of Enlightenment and the birth of colonialism, where man sought to have power over nature instead of living in harmony with it as our ancestors have always done. Where has that gotten us, but into an environmental and healthcare quagmire of destruction and addiction?

Since cannabis is a sacrament connected to divinity, we may be better served by communicating with the entire plant and seeking its guidance directly, rather than stripping and dismantling it into its isolated components in a lab, in order to see where its "real" power lies.

While dismantling cannabis in a lab may feel comforting to the scientific community because that's what they do, science isn't God. Deconstructing and synthesizing the plant in a lab isn't the only way to understand and use all of its vast potential.

In fact, I recommend any scientist interested in deconstructing any sacred medicine in a lab, first sit with it ceremonially for a few months. This time can be spent with the express intention to receive guidance from the sacrament itself about how best to analyze it and discover the different levels of wisdom it holds.

What might happen if we took a different approach to deconstructing the plant and instead sought out which strain evoked compassion? Which terpene might help create peace within a relationship instead of domestic violence? What if we strove to determine which aspect of the plant is best for unifying consciousness to achieve world peace and environmental health or for awakening your brain to lead you to your higher calling?

Most would agree that cannabis is effectively used to lessen anxiety and pain, but how many in the growing cannabis industry have considered packaging the plant's potential for elevating human consciousness and achieving peace and prosperity on a thriving planet? What about its history of use during funeral rites? What if we consulted the plant to determine how best to help those who are grieving? Suppressed grief is a huge cause of mental, emotional and physical health, and cannabis could do wonders to help process grief. But these issues aren't considered by a scientific community focused only on what they think they can "see" with their physical eyes, not what they can "see" with their intuition and heart, intimately guided by the sacraments themselves.

Is the aggressive drive to isolate compounds to the microcellular level truly honoring this plant teacher or is it a race for multinational businesses to be the first to create a patented cannabis synthetic compound to be sold for the greatest profit?

Many people use the manufactured edible products because the dosage is scientifically controlled. However, the best way to control the dosage when using cannabis and other psychedelic medicines is to communicate directly with the spirit teachers within. It's your birthright to send and receive communication from cannabis because of the endocannabinoid system and the Celestial Information Superhighway. Even though this isn't the type of information available at your hometown cannabis dispensary, it's available to you if you choose to access it. Again, the only thing that can get in the way of this communication is your self-doubt.

When you connect directly with the sacred medicine spirits and ask *them* for guidance and to show you the correct dosage for you on any given day, you're honoring their knowledge and allowing them to usher you toward the healing and expansion you desire. This is how ancient cultures revered the plants and followed their

Ceremonies of Sacred Life

wisdom from the dawn of time. It's a much more holistic use of the plants and keeps you from being manipulated by industrial marketing dollars.

CHAPTER 6: COSMORGASMIC ENERGY

Now let's talk about the elephant in the ceremony room: sexuality.

In some medicine circles the expression of sexual energy is welcomed. In other circles, it's considered disrespectful. The Divine Mother would like you to know that She has no judgement on your expression of sexual energy, but it's important to be respectful of the rules and boundaries of the medicine circle you're in. Disrespecting the rules and boundaries of your circle creates distractions for the participants and unnecessary work for the facilitation team, both of which take away from the experience and wisdom the sacred medicines are offering you.

She wants you to understand that orgasmically charged cosmic energy, or cosmorgasmic energy, is divine creation energy and is the pure root of existence. If you've ever felt a shimmery, vibrational quality to the DMT visions you've seen in ceremony, that vibrational quality is cosmorgasmic energy. Humans are used to channeling orgasmic energy purely for sexual intercourse, but it has a far greater potential than that. It's a pathway to higher knowledge, translated through your body.

Cosmorgasmic energy is the most powerful energy on the planet. It's a sacred expression of divinity and a vehicle the Divine

Mother uses for healing. Because it's so dynamic, orgasmic and ecstatic, it can easily go haywire in a ceremonial setting.

Considering Abstinence

Many psychedelic medicine circles recommend sexual abstinence before and after ceremony as part of their recommended preparation for doing the deep work. The main reasoning behind abstinence is to keep the energy field intact. What does that mean exactly?

Sexual energy is incredibly dynamic, and orgasm, whether alone or with a partner, requires significant release of that energy. Doing sacred medicine work also requires the use of vital energy, so by abstaining from sex around ceremony, your Human Energy System will have more vital energy to devote to the interdimensional healing process.

Also consider that orgasm is a total reset to the Human Energy System. It can shift your mental focus, change your mood and cause a variety of changes within the endocrine and cardiovascular systems. When you work with the psychedelic medicines, they help clear issues that are holding you back mentally and emotionally. Since orgasm can do much the same thing, you may be lessening the intensity of your mental and emotional issues post-orgasm, before you get to ceremony.

But wait! Isn't that a good thing?

Well, yes and no. When it comes to working with the sacraments, the more healing you're available for, the more healing you'll receive. For many people, abstaining from sex brings mental and emotional issues front of mind so to speak, and keeps them there, without release. By abstaining from orgasmic release before ceremony, you may feel more frustrated, anxious and irritable than normal, but it's this very state that that can allow the medicine to dig deeper for more healing than would have been possible if you'd had an orgasmic release to feel calmer and diffuse the anxiety and frustration.

Also, when we feel sexual desire, we often direct it outward to others. The innate cosmorgasmic energy that's part of the Human Energy System can get mistranslated toward another person, rather than being channeled within, for personal healing, which is how it's used by the sacred medicines.

Another reason that many medicine circles recommend sexual abstinence is because it's a way to strengthen self-will. Sexual energy is created inside of you. In reality, it has nothing to do with anyone else, which is why it can be channeled through sacred medicine work. We often turn to sexual fantasy and release for a sense of validation, to relieve a sense of insecurity or to escape reality, rather than keeping that energy within and using it for reflection and healing.

Based on my experience as a sex, love and relationships coach, many people carry around deeply buried sexual wounding, often going back generations and linked to cultural atrocities. These buried sexual wounds can be connected to repressed memories and experiences that create ongoing negative states, which unconsciously motivate daily actions and relationship choices. If those negative states are usually relieved by orgasm, it eliminates the opportunity for the core issues to be completely revealed and healed, which is what the sacred medicines can do.

SEXUAL PROJECTIONS

The Divine Mother wants to teach you that all true healing is expressed through ecstatic, cosmorgasmic energy at the cellular level. If you experience a profoundly ecstatic experience during a psychedelic medicine journey, honor that. Journal about it and see how you can translate that ecstasy into your day-to-day life. Remember that the quality of this energy doesn't have to be channeled through sexual intercourse. It can be any expression of creativity, joy, bliss and ecstasy. As long as you're honoring the boundaries of your circle and you're in alignment with kindness, compassion, plus your own and other people's boundaries and consent, the expression of cosmorgasmic energy is entirely up to you.

One of the most consistent experiences reported from being in sacred ceremonies is heart-opening. Sacred medicines create an incredibly loving space for interaction and growth. It's from this space that many people receive messages about getting in touch with lost loves, healing current romantic relationships or starting new romantic relationships, often with other ceremony participants.

The Divine Mother would like you to know that unless you receive a direct message to take immediate action, it's best to wait a few days or at least 24 hours to move forward with deeply loving and/or sexual feelings that come up during ceremony.

Remember the deepest healing happens at the cosmorgasmic level, which is ecstasy in vibration. Most humans aren't used to living day-to-day, vibrating that level of energy, so they automatically want to channel it into sex, when that may not be the best use of it. She suggests that you sit with the energy and breathe it through your body for a few days. Use deep breathing to experience the cosmorgasmic energy inside your body as it continues to heal you. If after that, you still feel called to move forward in sexual union with another, acting from a more grounded space will always yield better results. For more information about breathing sexual energy through your body, look into tantra or Taoist sexual practices.

The sacraments tend to bring up projections, or false representations of others inside of you. In other words, you may experience another person not as they are, but as you perceive them, altered by the sacred medicine weaving its way through you. In the worst cases, you can project your primordial, unhealed mother or sister issues onto a woman participant, or your primordial, unhealed father or brother issues onto a male participant. I've witnessed this repeatedly as a guardian.

In my main circle, those who identified as either male or female sat separately, and male-identified guardians tended to the male side, while female-identified guardians tended to the female side. Occasionally I offered healing to a man who was struggling through a rough passage because there weren't enough male guardians available to help him. A couple of times, it backfired on me because the man had deep unhealed mother wounds.

Once in particular, I felt attacked, and he felt disrespected. It took some time and communication for both of us to understand each other and return to a loving place. This is the type of challenge that can come up between genders, which is why it pays to be careful about the actions you take while still under the influence of the medicine.

If you're seeking a new mate and hoping to find them at ceremony, beware of the energy you're projecting. I've seen ungrounded people who didn't realize how much they oozed desperate sexual energy, and others who thought they were just "being friendly," but in reality, were relentlessly invading others' boundaries with their needy sexual desire.

It's safe to say that whatever is unhealed inside of you will be multiplied in ceremony by the sacred teachers and projected outwards. If you're asked by ceremony staff to back off, tone down the sexual energy or cover up your body, please receive these requests with humility and consider doing healing work around your sex, love and relationship issues. The more stable and grounded you are when you show up to ceremony, the better chance you'll have of magnetizing a great love, if that's your honest and heartfelt desire.

EROTIC BODY PRAYER

While the common guidance around ayahuasca is that sexual energy is to be conserved prior to ceremony, the guidance is different for psychedelic medicines that have known aphrodisiac qualities. Most notably, these are cannabis and psilocybin, but there are many sacred medicines known around the world, and certainly many of them have components that arouse sexual desire. Because of this, it's possible to use certain sacraments to awaken the cosmorgasmic energy within you and use it to communicate directly with the Celestial Beings and/or source consciousness itself.

"How does one do this?" you may be asking. It's easy. Just create an *Erotic Body Prayer* ritual!

Erotic Body Prayer is the name I give to the process that uses orgasmic sensations in your physical body to communicate directly with the divine, or source consciousness. Erotic Body Prayer requires that you move your left-brain consciousness out of the way so that your right brain/intuitive side can run the show for a while. You can reach a higher orgasmic state with breathwork alone and especially with tantric and Taoist sexual breathing techniques, but sacred medicines themselves however, are also a wonderful vehicle for expanding your consciousness to reach highly aroused, orgasmic states via cosmic energy, in order to facilitate communication with the Celestial Beings.

The most important caveat here is to set an intention. In other words, when working with aphrodisiac sacraments, it's your intention that helps usher you into alternate dimensions where you can communicate with source consciousness while highly orgasmically aroused.

Yes, it's really possible.

I recommend that you approach Erotic Body Prayer in the same way that you approach any psychedelic sacrament: with deep reverence and pure, loving intention. Based on my historical research as well as the experiments I've done in my own private lab (so to speak), I believe that Erotic Body Prayer was used for growth, transformation and divination in the ancient mystery schools across the world, especially considering that cannabis is a known aphrodisiac, its use can be traced back at least 10,000 years and there's evidence it was used for sacred and medicinal purposes consistently throughout that time.

Because the cosmorgasmic energy that can be awakened through psychedelic sacraments is so powerful, I strongly recommend that you set a ritual space and call in your spirit guides and protectors when doing Erotic Body Prayer. Have a benevolent intention for yourself and/or for higher service. Then you just proceed as you would in a more traditional type of medicine ceremony, only with the added benefit of highly aroused sexual energy circulating through your body.

This is not the time to get caught up in sexual fantasy around another person, especially someone that you aren't already in a sexual relationship with. As I mentioned, sexual energy is the most potent force in the universe, and combined with psychedelic medicines, it's not something to be trifled with or used for manipulation. You may think that sexual fantasy is harmless, but when you view it through the lens of sexual energy being the most potent force in the universe down to the microcellular level, it's anything but harmless.

If you cannot stay out of sexual fantasy around other people while attempting this work, then you aren't yet ready for it. Of course it's natural to think about a lover when your body is sexually activated - I'm not saying this is an easy process. However, I cannot emphasize enough that Erotic Body Prayer is extraordinarily powerful spiritual work and I caution you to approach it with the reverence it deserves. If you find yourself stuck in a sexual fantasy about another person in the middle of an Erotic Body Prayer ritual, just guide your mind back to a centered place and focus on source consciousness. At its seed level, this is a prayer and meditation practice and an opportunity for you to communicate with source consciousness in a way that isn't available to you in a normal, waking state. If you choose to do an Erotic Body Prayer with a lover, make sure they're congruent with your intentions so you can both be aligned in this consecrated work.

The Divine Mother wishes you to know that She is alive within you as you do Erotic Body Prayer, so you can use this work as a time to communicate with Her directly. She has no discrimination around what you do with another consenting adult, nor is She concerned about gender, sexual preferences or fetishes, as long as what you do is focused on your highest good. She is one

Ceremonies of Sacred Life

with cosmorgasmic energy, which is pure and free of societal and religious judgments and dogma. She is the vibrational force that lives inside of you, and She welcomes you to do this level of work with her, if you are ready.

CHAPTER 7: BEFORE & DURING CEREMONY – PRACTICAL TIPS

No matter which spirit teachers you commune with, there are certain themes that unfold with the energy around ceremony. The psychedelic medicines operate on the astral realm, so as soon as you make a commitment to go to ceremony, your life may begin to shift through subtle and not so subtle changes. Pay attention to any shifts you notice and use them as an opportunity to prepare for lessons you'll be receiving in ceremony.

Before Ceremony

THE CEREMONIAL JOURNAL

I suggest keeping a separate journal for your medicine ceremonies so that as soon as you decide to go to ceremony, you can begin journaling about your feelings. You can use all that information to facilitate integration and as a record of where you were and how you've changed over time since working with the medicine.

You may find that the life issues you're unhappy about start to become more present and/or intense in the days leading up to ceremony. This is your unconscious mind bringing up your life issues so the medicine can clear them. In your journal, record why you want to go, how you're feeling, what conflicts are present and what you hope to receive from ceremony. This allows your mind to be clear when you arrive to ceremony. In the Resources section, I share the journaling system I've developed over time and a list of questions to journal about before going to ceremony.

DIETAS

More than likely, the circle you're sitting with has a prescribed *dieta* (pre-ceremony diet) that's been handed down within that medicine lineage. The dieta is designed to help participants receive the medicine as deeply and healthfully as possible. The state of your body and mind determine how effectively the medicine can cleanse and heal you. If you do an online search of "ayahuasca diet," for example, you'll see that there's plenty of conflicting information. To eliminate confusion, I recommend sticking with the instructions for the particular group you're sitting with.

Also consider your personal physical tolerance. What are your general dietary and sleep needs? What's your level of tolerance with dietary supplements, for example? I'm highly sensitive to many supplements and food additives, an extremely light sleeper because of my sleep disorder and (no big surprise), I'm highly

Before & During Ceremony

sensitive to all sacraments. In my Human Energy System, a little goes a long way, but I've met many participants of all shapes and sizes who have a high tolerance for the sacred medicines.

If you know you have a sensitive constitution, it's important to get enough sleep and keep a diet that grounds you in the days leading up to ceremony. If you have a hard time with fasting, that's another reason to ensure you sleep well and keep a good diet during the days leading up to the ceremony and certainly the day of. Make no mistake, this is hard work, so you want to come well-rested and prepared to manage your experience.

It's also important to stay hydrated in the days leading up to the ceremony. At the very least, make sure you drink plenty of water the day of. When it comes to ayahuasca, make certain you're extra hydrated before ceremony starts because drinking water while on the medicine can make you purge from your stomach.

In the same way, your state of mind when you arrive at ceremony will determine your experience. Journaling your thoughts and feelings will help clear your mind and better prepare you for the experience. Most practitioners discuss what to eat before ceremony, but not many discuss what to think! Your dieta is your body diet and clearing your thoughts is your mind diet. Keeping both as clean as possible sets you up for the best ceremonial experience.

INTEGRATION

Do you have a plan to integrate the changes that will happen to you? The word "integration" is tossed around in the psychedelic medicine world, but what does it mean exactly? When you seek wisdom from the sacraments, your consciousness is deconstructed and then reconstructed, so to speak. You see and experience things that are way outside your normal reality. As I said earlier, the sacraments open the doors of perception to expanded consciousness. You will be different after communing with them. *Integration* is the process of bringing your up-leveled personality, behavior and new awareness into ecological harmony with your day-to-day life.

Psychedelic medicine experiences are specially designed for you to aid your soul's process of enlightenment. The Divine Mother wants you to know that because they're so far outside of normal reality, it can be challenging to hang onto what you've learned, especially if you don't act on the lessons. When you don't take time and energy to integrate your experiences, you set yourself up for confusion, instability and discomfort when you're back in your normal life routine. That discomfort can motivate you to turn right around and come back into ceremony. While we live on a free-will planet and you can keep coming back to the sacred medicines in an un-integrated state, it's not the best use of the medicine and you're doing yourself and the Divine Mother a disservice. Many people become untethered and lost because they approach the psychedelic medicines this way. They feel very light and "spiritual," but they're unable to implement those spiritual changes to create a more balanced, harmonious, grounded and compassionate life, which is what you, the Divine Mother and the planet need most of all.

The best use of the medicine is to integrate the psychedelic wisdom into your daily life and allow it to influence the words you choose, the company you keep, the business decisions you make and the way you interact with your loved ones. Staying linked up with the psychedelic wisdom is the way we'll uplift the entire planet.

Your Support System

Do you have a support group to turn to after ceremony to help you integrate? If you don't, consider creating one or finding a psychedelic integration coach or a spiritual counselor to help you. If you're comfortable with traditional therapy, just be advised that most therapists don't have psychedelic medicine experience, so they may need some education about your experience. See the Resources section for help with finding a psychedelic integration specialist.

Another way to make integration easier is to plan for it. Planning your integration process *before* ceremony, yields the best results. If possible, take time off before ceremony to prepare yourself and again after ceremony, to move gently through your integration process. The best thing you can do is spend as much time in nature as possible. Whatever it takes, I invite you to get some time around the natural world to help you ease back into your life. Also focus on walks, baths, exercise, spending time with pets or whatever self-care means to you.

Avoid jumping right back into 3-D world immediately after ceremony. For example, don't plan on running a bunch of errands or going to a big party on the way home from ceremony. I also recommend avoiding large family gatherings right after ceremony. Family is notorious for bringing up issues, so unless you have a magnificent family that's skillful with offering love, acceptance and support, it's best to avoid anything that may activate uncomfortable emotions within you. All senses are heightened for a few days after ceremony, so be gentle with yourself.

Planning Ahead

When considering a medicine ceremony, some of the most questions to ask are:

- What are the facilitator's qualifications?
- Do they regularly do their own healing work?
- Are they connected to an indigenous lineage?
- How will the ceremonial medicine be prepared?
- What exactly is in it?

- How does the facilitator determine the dosage per participant?
- Is there a recommended pre-ceremony diet?

Ask about the accommodations at the ceremony site so you know what to bring for your own comfort in the ceremony space. For example, will you need your own mat, pillows, blankets and meditation chair or will all those items be supplied by the group you're sitting with? What's the weather like and will you need to dress in layers or are there other clothing items you'll need?

Will food be provided? If so, what is it? Some groups have everyone bring a dish for the whole group to share. That's a generous gesture, but there's no way to know what you'll get. Because of my medical condition, I have a specific diet that I stick to in order to keep my brain functioning properly. I learned the hard way that the type of food provided at most ceremonies does not work for my digestion. I can't tell you how many times I've had a miserable evening ceremony after eating the food that was provided by well-meaning ceremony staff and participants. Now I bring a dish to share that I know works for my digestion and I also bring my own food in a cooler that I keep for myself. The last thing you need during a ceremony weekend is the distraction of excessively low blood sugar or an upset stomach, so plan ahead.

Planning ahead is especially important if you're attending ceremony internationally. If something goes wrong, you can't just walk out the door and go home. Check on whether or not you'll have an interpreter and what type of support you'll have before and after ceremony if you need it.

During Ceremony

Every ceremony circle has its own set of guidelines, so make sure you're clear about them before ceremony starts. Be aware of your SET (your state of mind) and SETTING (the ceremonial space itself).

When it comes to setting, there are a few things to consider. If the facilitators are experienced, you should feel comfortable and safe in the ceremony space. They should be checking in with you to see how you are and making sure you know what to expect in ceremony.

SAFETY

If you feel anything weird or uncomfortable, absolutely trust it unequivocally! That's your intuition talking and there's no better indicator of safety than your intuition. Bring up any concerns you have to the facilitators and make sure they do whatever they can to rectify the situation. Here's where it gets tricky: sometimes being uncomfortable is part of anticipating the sacred medicine experience. It may be hard to tell if you're anxious and afraid of

Before & During Ceremony

having uncomfortable things revealed to you by the sacrament, or if the setting itself is unsafe.

If the facilitators cannot rectify what you feel is an unsafe situation before ceremony starts and you're legitimately in fear for your personal safety, then leave. Don't worry about what someone else might think! You may end up losing some deposit money, but your personal safety is priceless and there's no reason to take a chance with it, ever.

A caveat here – if you've already taken a dose and you're under the influence of medicine, it's not safe to leave or drive. Wait until the effects of the medicine have worn off before you leave.

However, if the facilitators are willing to carefully address your concerns and make sure you feel comfortable and safe and yet you still feel uneasy, it could be that your fears are coming up before you take the sacrament. In this case, see if you can pinpoint exactly what's causing your anxiety and fear. Get as clear on this as you possibly can and meditate on it before you receive the sacrament, to settle your mind.

Next, do an energy shielding exercise to clear your energetic space. This is a good time to call in any angels, spirit guides and/or ancestors to protect you during the ceremony. Remember, there are entities present when people are purging and clearing their consciousness, so it never hurts to have extra protectors in your corner. See the Resources section for a simple energy shielding exercise.

Focusing Your Intentions & Prayers

In Chapter 4: How the Medicines Work, I introduced the concept of intentions and prayers. During ceremony is the time to put them to use. Hopefully by the time the ceremony starts, you've written down your intentions and prayers in your ceremony journal, or you've recorded them somewhere for reflection later.

When you're in ceremony with a group, there's usually a period of time when people are milling about and talking before the official opening of ceremony. This is a good time for you to turn your thoughts inward and reflect upon your intentions and prayers, so you have them memorized before the medicine takes effect.

Once the medicine takes effect, your consciousness will expand and depending upon the type and strength of sacrament you're receiving, you may have a sense that the world is dissolving around you. Having your intentions clear ahead of time will benefit you during strong passages, especially when you're experiencing an intense amount of psychedelic visuals and claircognizance.

Remember that claircognizance is the ability to acquire knowledge without knowing how or why you know it. You just KNOW. DMT and psychedelic activation ushers in a deep transmission of wisdom, which you may experience as claircognizance. When visions and claircognizance happen together, the powerful combination can cause uncomfortable physical feelings. This is probably when you'll be feeling most "out of your mind," and needing to purge.

Before & During Ceremony

The Divine Mother wants you to know that this is the time you're receiving her wisdom most intensely. If you get scared or concerned, do your best to breathe deeply and put your focus back on your intentions and prayers and that focus will ground you.

DISTRACTIONS

Because you're in an altered state of consciousness during ceremony, the slightest energetic shift can create a distraction for you and others. Distractions can throw you off course, which is why a good facilitator will give instructions before the ceremony starts about how to minimize them. However, managing distractions starts with managing yourself.

Think of the ceremonial space as a sacred temple. As soon as you enter, slow your movements down. Allow yourself to feel calm and peaceful, even if you have to fake it till you make it. Remove your shoes (if appropriate) and walk gently and quietly the entire time you're in the temple space; before, during and after ceremony. Loud, heavy walking can be a distraction to others, so be conscious about how you move.

Also consider your voice. It's best to avoid any conversation whatsoever during ceremony, but if you must communicate vocally, do so in a lowered tone and whisper, which are the best possible ways to avoid distracting anyone else with your conversation.

Use the entrance of the ceremonial temple as a signal to lower your voice. The more often you do ceremony, the more you'll notice how a person's tonality and voice register have an energy that's easy to feel. Speaking in your normal "outside voice" register is one of the most jarring distractions in the ceremonial space and can easily take someone out of their deep visionary experience, so be mindful and conscious about speaking in quiet tones.

Since the sacred medicines activate love and oneness, people often want to hug each other during ceremony. It's a natural human response to want to comfort someone who's suffering or to express feelings of love, but it's best to override those urges during ceremony.

Remember that the sacraments bring up deep emotions and life issues to be revealed and healed, so people often look like they're suffering. This is a normal part of the process, and a good facilitation staff will be on top of it. If you're honestly concerned about someone's safety, speak to a ceremony guardian or the facilitator. Don't interact directly with the person who's going through a rough passage. Interrupting someone with talk or touch may interrupt the healing they're receiving.

In one of my ceremonies, I was outside crying, in the middle of a deep healing around issues with my son. As I was receiving these deep insights, one of the male participants walked over to me, grabbed my arm and said, "Are you okay? Do you need some help?" It pulled me right out of the Divine Mother's guidance, and it took several seconds before I could even respond to the man. I was so rattled, all I could do is shake my head, "no." His approach was so jarring that to this day I don't remember what the Divine

Mother was showing me. I know this man was goodhearted and meant well, but his actions did more harm than good.

Expectations

One of the biggest hurdles that people new to ceremony must overcome is their expectations. Many people do excessive online research before ceremony and then show up expecting something specific, or the same experience that a friend had. If someone is confused or disappointed after ceremony, nine times out of ten it's because they had specific expectations for ceremony that weren't met, or this ceremony was different than their last and they're unhappy about it or feel a loss of control.

Every single psychedelic medicine is different, and every single ceremony is different - because YOU are different. Your physiology and emotional state change all the time. The Human Energy System is fluid and evolving and that's what the sacred medicines react to.

The Divine Mother wishes to remind you that when you agree to receive a sacrament, you agree to receive Her wisdom. It comes in its own way, outside of your control. There's a process you need to go through in the total arc of your healing and enlightenment. Certain layers must unfold before others. This is a process designed outside of human consciousness. There's NO WAY to predict what the sacred medicines have in store for you on your pilgrimage of compassionate enlightenment. Releasing expectations of any specific outcome will put you at ease and give you the best ceremonial experience overall.

Sailing Through Rough Passages

This brings us to the point in the book that answers the question most people have: "How do I keep from freaking out when the medicine takes over?"

My usual answer is, "Why is it a problem? Maybe you're supposed to freak out."

But I get it. It's a concern. Here are some practical tips to navigate rough passages that make you question why the hell you decided to ingest the sacrament in the first place.

First off, stay seated upright. Even though in that uncomfortable moment, it may feel like the hardest thing you've ever done, when you sit upright, your spine is erect, and your airways are more open than they are when your body is collapsed. This simple act alone will help you maintain your composure, so unless you have express instructions otherwise from the sacred medicine, sit upright and don't curl up into the fetal position.

Secondly, breathe, breathe, breathe! Breathing deeply and remaining seated through a hard passage can be challenging, but it's the best thing you can do for yourself. It will help you stay grounded as you receive the wisdom, and it can also help with the urge to purge. As you go to more ceremonial circles, you may notice that the experienced people spend most of their time sitting up and breathing because they've learned that it's the best and easiest way to receive wisdom from the sacraments, while managing any nausea or other discomfort.

Purging

Another common thing people new to the medicine say is, "I'm afraid to throw up." In my experience, this is the number one reason why people resist taking sacred medicines, especially ayahuasca. Well, guess what? Luckily, there's some good news for you: there's more than one way to purge!

The purpose of purging is to purify your heart and spirit. This purification isn't something that can easily be done in your waking life because your Human Energy System overrides you going into a deep purification like this. There are a few exceptions of course, one of which is deep breathing work and/or deep emotional releases, which can happen without the help of psychedelic medicines.

Physical purging can happen through tears, laughter, coughing, yawning, breathing, shaking, moaning/vocalizing, from the stomach (referred to as vomiting), through energetic release (similar to dry heaving), peeing and also through the bowels (defecating and passing gas). There are probably other ways to purge as well, so be ready for anything.

In my first ceremony, I was as afraid of purging from my stomach as any other newcomer. When I felt it happening, I felt incredible physical discomfort of course, but as soon as I purged, I felt an immense sense of emotional lightness and release and I'm so glad it happened. After that first purge from the stomach, in my decade of ceremonial work, I've probably only purged from my stomach a handful more times. I purge in a variety of other ways, and every ceremony is different. Your experience will be different, too. That's why the best approach to purging is to welcome it! Remember, you're not "getting sick" in your bucket – you're getting well. And that's one of the biggest benefits of working with the sacred medicines in the first place, isn't it?

How to Know If The Dosage is Correct

The key to finding the correct dosage of sacrament is to take enough so you can't resist the process, but don't take so much that you're unable to remember what happened. On occasion, I've taken large doses of medicine that set me up for out-of-control, scary rides. Anyone who works with psychedelic medicines long enough, probably has similar stories to tell. While psychedelic medicine journeys can be confusing to integrate in the best of situations, it's not safe to be overdosed.

Every ceremony circle is different, so check in with the facilitator about how they determine dosage. In some circles, everyone is given a similar dose at first and in other circles, the dosage is subjective and based on interactions between the facilitator and each participant. In my main circle, the facilitator determined dosage based on conversations with each participant and the type of experience they wanted. One of the most common questions that came up was, "How do I know how much medicine to ask for?" My answer was always the same: "Ask the Divine Mother."

That's still the best advice I can give. Communicate directly with the spirit teachers and trust the information they give you. Remember that everyone has their own special connection with the Divine Mother and with the spirit teachers. If you can trust your intuition, you can trust the communication you receive from the sacraments.

To communicate directly with the spirit teachers, simply get into a quiet, meditative state and imagine that you're connecting with their energy. Simply ask them what dosage they recommend for you and pay attention to the first thing that comes up in your mind. I realize this is easier said than done for people unaccustomed to working with their intuition, so be sure to have this communication while in the ceremonial space, not far ahead of time. If the ceremonial space is set up with integrity, you can connect with the spirit of the medicine before it's offered to you. If this is all new to you, allow yourself to trust the process. Between the intuitive information you receive and the guidance you get from your facilitator, you'll have the correct dosage.

Also remember that the ceremony is only part of your overall experience and healing. Much can be revealed as your mind expands prior to ceremony, in talk circle after the ceremony and then over the next few days as the sacrament continues to weave through you. If all else fails, remember that a dose of psychedelic medicine rarely lasts more than a few hours. If you're honestly having a confusing, scary and challenging experience, ask for help! Also remember that the journey is temporary. You'll live through it and eventually be at peace on the other side.

MUSIC

Traditionally, music and sound healing are integral parts of ayahuasca and other sacred medicine ceremonies. A skilled facilitator will use a variety of songs and chants throughout the ceremony, to set the tone of the ceremony, move through different passages and facilitate healing and purging among other things. Many of the songs used in ayahuasca and other sacred medicine ceremonies are called *icaros*, which are songs shamans receive directly from the sacraments themselves. Icaros have a magical ability to shift consciousness, no matter in which language they're sung.

When you're under the influence of sacred medicine, the songs can be your travel companions and show you deep wisdom, while offering healing. If you're stuck in a dark or challenging place during ceremony, turn to the music being offered and lean into it. Breathe it in and it will ground you and help with your ceremonial experience. Many songs are designed to be sung as a group, so if you hear other people singing along, you can too! Even if you don't know the words, you can hum along, to stay in deep contact with the medicine of the music.

Some facilitators open up a special time in the latter part of the ceremony for anyone interested to offer a song. If this opportunity presents itself and you're inspired to take it, keep in mind that you're *offering a prayer* through song, not staging a performance from ego. Remember that all vibration in ceremony can be magnified, so come from your heart when offering a prayer through music. Unless you're invited to offer a song, allow the ceremony staff to organize the musical offerings and just lean back and receive them.

TALK CIRCLE

Talk circle or talking circle is a traditional indigenous way of sharing information from the heart. Some call it "healing through feeling." Many (but not all) psychedelic medicine lineages hold a talk circle after the ceremony. Some open the circle immediately after ceremony and some open it the next morning, after the participants have had time to rest. There are enormous benefits from participating in talk circle, not the least of which is the opportunity to experience how there's a connection between everyone in ceremony. I've had massive growth from talk circles alone, which is one of the reasons I know how important they can be.

The Divine Mother would like you to understand the importance of talk circles to facilitate healing and integration of the sacred medicine wisdom. She asks that you make yourself available for talk circle if one is offered. Do whatever you can to plan your time so that you can remain with the group until talk circle is complete. This one small act will be a great contribution toward elevating humanity and increasing enlightenment through sacred medicine work.

Follow the guidelines for talk circle and be respectful of others. Each lineage has a system for talking that usually allows one person to speak at a time. Speak from your heart and not your head, stay focused on your ceremony experience (not the rest of your life story) and be courageous enough to be vulnerable and authentic in what you share. Not only will it help you, but it may also help someone else in the circle who needs to hear about *your* experience for their own healing.

If your lineage doesn't offer a talk circle after ceremony, either get together with some of the other participants to create your own circle or spend some time alone after ceremony (preferably in nature) to record your thoughts and experiences in your ceremony journal.

CHAPTER 8: AFTER CEREMONY

How to Live an Intentional Life

So, you survived your psychedelic medicine ceremony. Congratulations! Now what the heck do you do? The Divine Mother would like you to remind you that ayahuasca and other spirit teachers may not heal you in the way you expect them to. Their transmission of knowledge is non-linear and multi-dimensional and outside of what the logical mind is used to. Because of this, you may find yourself confused or unsure if you're properly integrating the changes in yourself after ceremony. If you're in a state of confusion, it's a perfect time to get out your ceremony journal and review the messages you received. They may make more sense in the fullness of time.

As I said previously, the best thing you can do for yourself after ceremony is to get out in nature as much as possible. Being in touch with the natural world is good for the mind, body and spirit and a good walk outside amongst the grass, trees and flowers is known for setting the mind at ease. Whenever I'm in an anxious state and I need to make a decision, I go for a walk to discharge some of the energy I'm feeling so I can communicate more effectively. Between being in nature and working with your ceremonial journal, you'll be able to translate your insights and integrate them into your life.

The changes you notice after ceremony will vary from big to small. Your conscious mind may try to convince you that the wisdom you received wasn't "real" because it didn't happen in a rational, linear way. However, people in your life will probably notice something different about you, so use that feedback to help convince your conscious mind that the otherworldly experiences were valid and they really did happen.

After ceremony, you'll probably have ideas and insights about actions you should take. Pay attention. The number one most important thing you can do to further your growth and healing is to take the recommended action! Don't sit back passively and let the moment for growth and healing pass. We live on a free-will planet and are ultimately responsible for our own growth, so the Divine Mother can only do so much. Don't waste your deep experience by going back to your old way of doing things once you've been given guidance on how to improve your life.

Hints about further actions you need to take can come in as signs around you, snippets of conversation you hear, changes in your food cravings, a desire to drink less alcohol, eat less refined sugar or make other dietary changes. It could be an urge to have a conversation you've been avoiding or an urge to change your job, residence or partner. It could be anything, so keep an open mind and stay present! All the subtle and obvious changes you're experiencing are an outgrowth of the ceremony experience, so dismiss nothing. As one of my spiritual teachers says, "You can have anything you want, as long as you pay... *attention.*"

Paying attention to the messages you receive both in ceremony and afterwards, and then taking action on them are the building blocks of enlightenment. It can be that simple to translate interdimensional communication into your day-to-day life, so allow your life to be that simple and profound.

Own Your Stuff

As I mentioned, after ceremony you'll be feeling different than you did before. While you're in transition and making sense of what you learned from the sacred medicines, you may be in an agitated space from time to time, because as they say, "your stuff is up." That means certain things your friends and loved ones say and do may cause you to feel anger, anxiety or other negative emotions and then project those negative emotions outward back at them. If you find this happening to you, recognize that your repressed emotions, frustrations and challenges related to your own growth are very present and in your face. This can make you feel uncomfortable and sometimes lashing out at someone else seems like a solution in the moment, but it's a one-way ticket to blocking your growth and enlightenment.

If you find this happening, it's time to own your stuff! I invite you to act as if there's a higher purpose to what's happening. Your entire life unfolded to bring you into this moment, where you can make a massive life shift. Your discomfort is the shadow part of your identity and your courage to work with the medicine shines light on that shadow and allows liberation and light into your life and the lives of those who surround you.

Uncomfortable emotions are a great opportunity to go deeper into the healing offered by the sacred medicines, integrate it and anchor it in light. The process may not be all fun but being courageous and buckling down for the inner ride is much more rewarding than blaming others for the fact that your growth process isn't as glamorous as it could be.

Instead of lashing out at another, what you may need is physical exercise, meditation, reflection, prayer and/or some quiet time in nature with your ceremony journal. Do whatever it takes to feel your emotions, heal them and release them. Experiment with different self-care and soothing activities until you find some that help you get out of your discomfort and back into the open-hearted and compassionate place you probably were in when you left ceremony. The ceremony circle may seem far away in these moments, especially if you had your experience in a different country, but make no mistake, the medicine is inside of you. It's part of you and you always have a connection with the Divine Mother, so healing and guidance are always available to you from your connection with Her.

On the flipside, being committed to staying in your open heart isn't a substitute for doing your inner work and integration. Refusing to acknowledge negativity crossing your path is a spiritual bypass. Don't turn away from making difficult changes in your life because you're addicted to staying in that floaty, open-hearted, compassionate space you were in after ceremony. Staying in compassion is a clear path to enlightenment, but if you refuse to acknowledge mistakes you've made and refuse to resolve unhealthy situations in your life because you want to stay in the "love and light," you're not growing.

Psychedelic medicines can be harsh teachers and so can life itself. Be grounded and courageous and ask for guidance from the Divine Mother or the sacraments themselves about how to best move forward in a difficult situation.

If you don't already have a daily prayer and meditation practice, communing with the spirit teachers can be great motivation to start one. The groundedness of daily practice can do wonders as you move through your post-ceremony issues. See the Resources section for tips on starting a prayer and meditation practice.

Considerations For Your Loved Ones

If you recently came to an ayahuasca or another sacred medicine ceremony and your loved one is concerned because they think you're acting really weird, here are some tips to help you help them and help yourself.

First, let them know you're working through your issues. The changes in you may be very disconcerting to your loved one, so remember, they haven't experienced the life-altering, interdimensional rollercoaster ride you've just been on. They likely have no context for your experience.

If you head right in after ceremony to talk to them about seeing ancestors, the Celestial Beings and mystical animals and how you purged from every orifice and it was SO F-ING AMAZING, they may feel overwhelmed and threatened and start to get very worried about you and themselves as they maneuver through your confessionals.

I invite you to take a step back and lower the intensity of your communication. Save the juiciest bits for your ceremonial journal and for the people familiar with medicine work until your loved ones have gotten used to the new you. Once you've had time to settle into a new rhythm in your old life, slowly share bits of your ceremony experience as you see fit. You have plenty of time to do this – there's no deadline. Go slowly, continue to heal yourself and allow your loved ones to notice the subtle or not so subtle changes in you. When they point something out, you can acknowledge how it's an outgrowth of your ceremony experience. This will allow your loved ones to understand how the experience fits into all of your lives overall, without feeling isolated, threatened or left out because they weren't there with you. If it's possible for you, set aside time to process after ceremony before you see your loved ones again.

I have a great relationship with my son, and I share custody with his dad, so I have my son half the week and every other weekend. My main ayahuasca facilitators lived out of state and came to my area twice a year for about 8 weeks at a time, so of course I wanted to be available as often as possible while they were in town. Every time I went to ceremony on the weekends I had my son, I'd leave him with his dad or grandparents on Friday afternoon and then go straight from talk circle to pick him up on Sunday afternoon.

No matter how hard I tried to stay balanced and calm, we would fight every time I was with him right at the end of a ceremony weekend. Ceremony weekends can be exhausting, especially when you're head guardian *and* a light sleeper. Truth be told, I was so fatigued when I picked him up on Sunday afternoons, I wasn't in a good and patient space to turn right around from drinking ayahuasca to be earth-mom again.

After a few miserable Sundays like this, I stopped going to ceremony on the weekends I had him. As much as I wanted to do my sacred service every weekend, it simply wasn't workable in my life. My son was more important. I chose to make him the priority and I've never regretted that choice. Sometimes you need to make these types of decisions where your children and other loved ones are concerned, so consider your entire life and plan ahead for how you're going to land back into your life after ceremony. The Divine Mother wants you to know there's always a solution when it comes to receiving the sacraments. If now isn't the right time because of family commitments, another better time will arrive. As Frances Scovel Shinn says in her seminal book, *The Game of Life and How to Play It*, "Divine ideas never conflict."

If your own parents and loved ones are concerned about you going into ceremony, give them this short book to read and invite them to scan the Glossary of Terms and Resources section, so they know you're well educated on the ceremonial experience. There are many other books, articles and blog posts written by experienced medicine people. There's no reason for your loved ones to be worried about your safety if you share this information with them to help them know you're well protected. Sometimes it's easier to refer them to an expert rather than explain your decision in your own words.

Taking 3-D Action

Often, the shifts that happen during ceremony are so profound, when you leave the ceremonial space, you feel like it's time to blow up your life: break up with your partner, quit your job, move to a new location, sell your business or other drastic changes. The Divine Mother would like you to know that unless you receive exact guidance to make an immediate change for your personal safety, it's best to wait and settle back into your life before you make any big decisions. She reminds you that you're a divine being having a human experience, but you're still having a *human experience*. The most helpful way to grow and evolve for the highest good of all concerned is to bring the profound interdimensional wisdom you receive from the spirit teachers, back into your day-to-day life and allow it to percolate and integrate.

Any major decision is best made with thoughtfulness, compassion and an open heart. Sitting in prayer, meditation and reflection before you make a life-changing decision is always wise. The Divine Mother also reminds you that you can consult with Her anytime! This is why it's so vital to have a prayer and meditation practice, especially when receiving wisdom from the psychedelic medicines.

If you feel like you're going to go crazy unless you blow up your life, it's a good sign that you're out of balance. A common goal-setting technique is to focus on the *quality* of what you think the goal will bring you. For example, if you want a million dollars, it's not the stacks of currency that your heart desires, it's the freedom, luxury, vacations and change in lifestyle. that the million dollars will bring you.

Rather than lighting an incendiary device in your life, meditate on what the drastic change will bring you. When you gain clarity around the new qualities you desire, pray and meditate on ways to bring those qualities into your current life and then take action on the wisdom you receive. As you follow this process, you may find the challenging situation that you wanted to light a torch to, either doesn't look so bad after all, or diminishes on its own. The sacraments work in magical ways, and let's face it, they don't necessarily speak in your native tongue, so be open to multiple ways of receiving their communication.

Ceremonies of Sacred Life

Putting It All Together

Here's an example of how you can use what you've learned in this book before making a life-altering decision, prompted by communing with the spirit teachers:

- Record your insights from ceremony in your ceremonial journal, including the guidance you received around making a big decision or lifestyle change.
- Instead of making an immediate decision, keep the information to yourself, continue to write about it in your ceremonial (or other) journal and let the information process over a few days at least.
- Be in nature as much possible and continue to take care of yourself with a healthy diet, plenty of water and exercise.
- Keep a daily prayer and meditation practice to stay connected with the Divine Mother so you can continue to receive Her guidance while you contemplate your big decision.

- Bring the qualities into your life that you think the big life change will give you.
- Once you feel like you've received enough wisdom to decide with clarity and compassion, you move forward and take the necessary action with an open heart.

Do you see how different this process is, rather than coming home from ceremony and announcing that the psychedelic medicine "told" you to quit your job, pack up and move out with no plan in place? So many people have a deep, interdimensional experience with the spirit teachers and then become untethered from their lives and unhappy because all the magic they experienced didn't translate that easily into 3-D world and then they feel lost, confused and unsure about what's real and what isn't.

The Divine Mother reminds you that She's here for you and all can happen in right timing for the highest good of all. "Now" is just one point on the space-time continuum. As long as you're in flow with the sacrament and allowing it to weave consciously and reverently through your day-to-day life, you're honoring the great work, elevating yourself and becoming enlightened at the perfect time and in the perfect way for you and for the highest good of all

Ceremonies of Sacred Life

concerned, including you, your loved ones, the Divine Mother herself and planet earth.

CHAPTER 9: BLESSINGS TO YOU

When you live in your true purpose and expanded vibration, you become a living example of how others can live in compassion and oneness, not by what you say but by what you vibrate. Working with the spirit teachers awakens the possibility of bringing new frequencies into your life and holding them inside of your Human Energy System in order to guide you into a higher purpose.

The Divine Mother invites you to hold onto what She's shown you in this book, so you may remain aligned in the integrity of your soul's higher vibration. You can do this by living in a prayerful way that projects your frequency of light into all that you encounter. Living prayer is about having reverence for each moment. Infusing prayer and compassion into everything you do helps you surround yourself with objects, food, people and experiences that are of the light, while allowing whatever is out of harmony with your expanded vibration to fall away effortlessly. Living in a higher frequency of compassion is what the sacred medicine wisdom is teaching you.

The Divine Mother also invites you to remain connected with the interdimensional aspects of yourself that you're shown by the spirit teachers. When you remain aligned to this new way of living, it creates a new song in you that you can sing and share with the entire planet, simply by shifting and holding your new frequency. The more you believe and live in the knowledge the sacraments provide and release ego-heavy aspects of self that hold you in the past, the better chance you have of inspiring others. This is how we expand the paradigm of compassion and oneness for all instead of fear, manipulation and war.

As more humans link up with higher frequencies opened by the sacred medicines, the frequency of the planet shifts as a matter of course. Everything you do and say has an effect on Pachamama. You're that important.

And of course, you have free will. You're welcome to choose pain instead of joy, anger instead of compassion and ego instead of oneness. What you choose today will change the earth tomorrow. Relatives, I invite you to choose wisely.

May you be surrounded by the holy light of source consciousness as you feel in each moment how loved you are and how rare and special your unique vibration is now and ever will be. May you be showered with blessings as you move with ease and grace on your journey.

Blessings to you.

RESOURCES

SHIELDING TECHNIQUE

Intuition comes from the unconscious and higher conscious aspects of the Human Energy System, but we're used to operating in the world from the conscious mind, which is the part of us that gets things done.

I strongly suggest that anyone who works with the psychedelic medicines keeps a regular energetic shielding practice. I also invite you to do this technique the first thing every morning (which is what I do) and if you're highly empathic and sensitive to the energy of others, do it again before and after you're in crowds or emotionally charged situations.

As you approach this technique, be aware that imagination, the unconscious and intuition are all linked together. The more you can access all three with this exercise, the better, so play with it! Have fun and trust what you "see" in your mind's eye.

Remember that entities can be released when people purge, so it's always a good idea to set your own protective space on top of whatever protection your facilitators employ. I recommend doing this shielding exercise once you have your assigned space, but before ceremony begins.

- Settle into a calm space and take 5 deep breaths.
- Put your attention on your crown chakra (at the top of your head) and focus on your concept of a Higher Power.
- Now put your attention on your heart chakra (your heart area) and feel love pulsating in this area. If you need help connecting with heart energy, think of a loving moment from your past or a loving moment you look forward to in the future. Next, imagine the crown chakra at the top of your head opening up and a massive beam of light entering and flowing through you from above. This beam of light is from your Higher Power - from the highest levels of divine consciousness and it is completely benevolent.
- Imagine the beam of light shooting out of your heart and surrounding you entirely, as it loops back on itself.

- As it flows through you, imagine it cleansing your Human Energy System completely. It moves through your energetic field and physical body, clearing away any negativity, self-doubt and emotions from others.
- As this process continues, say to yourself, "I am surrounded by the highest, holy and sacred light, protected in all dimensions of space, time and matter. I am complete." The exact words here are not as important as the intention that you BELIEVE you deserve to be safe, and you have the ability to shield yourself from energies that aren't your own.
- Sit quietly in this vision for as long as you'd like. When you're finished, express gratitude to your Higher Power for support and protection.

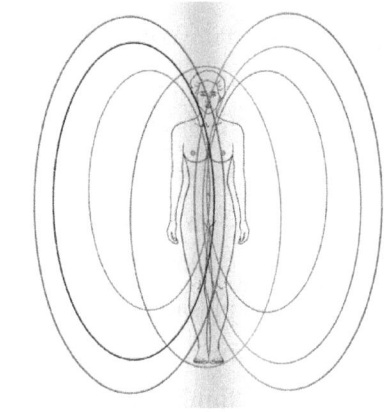

That's it! Do this as often as you'd like. The more often you do it, the easier it will be to manage your boundaries and stay grounded.

Food Prayers

There are two types of prayers I use for food – one for preparing food and one to bless my food before I eat it. I share these prayers with love and friendship. Feel free to adapt them for your own uses.

Preparing Food

This is adapted from a Mayan prayer I learned for gathering healing plants. Start with the quality you want to invoke for your meal as you prepare it. It could be friendship, forgiveness, love, peace, perfect health, or any other positive quality you desire more of. I keep a small sound bowl in my kitchen to begin and end this prayer, but you can use a bell or chime, or just say the prayer without the added sound healing.

"In the name of the Divine Mother, pure source energy, I give thanks to you, the spirit within this food and I have faith with all of my heart in your great healing and nourishing properties. I am (__insert your name__), here, holding the light. I bring the heart of my ancestors into this moment to prepare this food and transmit the highest vibrations for the planet." Then say the quality three times. For example, "Perfect health, perfect health, perfect health. And so it is."

While you're preparing your food, I invite you to do to stay in a positive mindset and focus on the quality you evoked in your invocation.

Before Eating Animal Products

No matter what you eat, an insect, rodent, bird, fish or 4-legged animal gave their life for your food. This prayer is an opportunity for you to connect with the spirit of those creatures and give thanks and blessings for their sacrifice. I start this prayer by bringing to mind the creatures(s) that I'm eating.

"Dear brother (or sister) (name of creature), thank you for giving your life for my (and/or my family's) health and nourishment. As our souls merge as one, may we both come to a higher level of enlightenment. I'm sorry if you suffered during your transition. Go in peace."

For a general blessing at the table, you can say something as simple as, "Thank you to anyone who had a hand in helping to create this meal. (This includes anyone in the agricultural industry who grew, picked and transported the food, as well as those preparing it for the table.) Bless, bless, bless!"

That's it!

CEREMONIAL JOURNAL QUESTIONS

Here are some questions to journal about before you attend ceremony, to make sure you're in the best state of mind to receive the sacraments. When you apply these questions to your medicine work, it will keep you grounded and will facilitate your ongoing integration process.

- Why specifically do you want to go to ceremony and what do you hope to see when you get there?
- What do you know about the indigenous roots of the medicine? What do you know about the indigenous peoples and lineages where these medicines come to us from?
- Have you released expectations of the ceremonial experience?
- Can you afford to pay for ceremony and the sacraments?
- Have you arranged for integration before you return to your close relationships?
- Are you taking the sacraments to gain a deeper understanding of life? If so,

what will you do with that deeper understanding?
- Are you willing to stand for the earth, for all people, for love?
- Are you coming to ceremony to make new friends and new connections? If so, what will you do with those connections?
- Have you done the homework assigned to you from your last experience?
- Are you making necessary changes in your life, to keep rising up in vibrational alignment?
- Are you considering going to back to ceremony because you feel uncomfortable in your life? If so, what efforts have you already made to change your current uncomfortable situation?

Ceremonial Journal Set-Up

The following is an example of how I set up my ceremonial journal. At the top of the page, I record the day and date and which ceremony it is: 1st, 2nd, 3rd, 10th, etc. I also record the dosage(s) and of course, my intentions and prayers.

If it's a new moon or full moon, I record that as well. I'm significantly affected by lunar cycles, and I've observed that most regular ceremony participants notice a different intensity with the medicines during lunar cycles. In addition, there's a six-month link between new and full moons. When a new moon falls in a particular zodiac sign, a full moon will be in the same zodiac sign approximately six months later. Each zodiac sign has a different energy signature, so tracking lunar cycles within the signs can reveal a common thread.

New moons are a great time to kick off new projects and create fresh starts. Full moons are good for completion and harvesting what you've created. When you track sacred ceremonies that take place during these lunar cycles, you can look back and see if the seeds you planted during the new moon are coming to fruition during the full moon in the same zodiac sign six months later.

Since the visions and insights from ceremony fade over time, I suggest that you do your very best to set up your journal ahead of time and then as soon as possible after the ceremony, write short snippets of the visions, feelings and insights no matter how tired you are. If you have the energy and brain capacity to tap into your left-brain conscious mind and actually write everything out after ceremony, that's best because all the events are top of mind and present. If you choose to fill out your journal completely right after ceremony, I invite you to go back the next day and review it, to make sure it makes logical sense. What seems clear when you're still slightly under the influence of psychedelic medicines, may not make sense in the light of day, hence the need for a quick review.

If you're too tired to write out all the insights before you go to sleep, make sure to at least write out the snippets of what you remember. That way, when you go back to your journal the next day, you can link up to the memories from the ceremony. Also, if you decide to write in the morning, I recommend you do it first thing before anything else, like checking email or getting on the phone. The more you get into your daily, left-brain waking life rhythms, the harder it is to access the unconscious mind right-brain visions and insights from ceremony.

As I'm recording what happened in ceremony, I often have thoughts pop in my head that I forgot to write down in the short snippets section. If this happens to you, I recommend writing those thoughts at the very top of the page, so you can continue writing and come back to them after you finish your current thought. This way you don't miss anything that cycles through your mind as you write. See example below.

Date: 3/10/22   New Moon in Scorpio
14th ayahuasca ceremony   2 doses

INTENTIONS & PRAYERS:
- Guidance about whether to quit my job
- How to communicate more compassionately with my son
- Prayers for my aunt Joyce, who's sick

NOTES TO FILL IN LATER:

Saw snake that guided me into the forest to help with communication.
DMT experience opened my heart – co-workers
Hummingbird showed me where my son's coming from
Felt wave of understanding for Aunt Joyce after 2nd dose
Purging during 1st dose showed me how blocked I am

[Once you're ready to fill in your journal, write your thoughts and memories on your journal pages.]

Resources

Subsequent Pages – [Recording Other Thoughts]

Got insights from looking at the stars, John communicated from other side, Jaguar after 2nd dose

[If thoughts pop in your head while you're writing in your journal, make a short note of them at the top of the page so you don't forget them. Then go back and fill in the details in your journal pages.]

How to Trust & Master Your Intuition

I have an entire course on intuition called "Bloom Your Intuition," which is a comprehensive system including videos and documents that teach how to build and use your intuition every day. You can access Bloom Your Intuition from my website: www.inthedivine.com/how-to-use-your-intuition

Here are some tips from that course that you can use right away.

First, I invite you to understand that intuition is your birthright! It's part of the non-physical aspect of your humanity. That means it's part of your Human Energy System. Everyone (including you) is born with a perfectly working intuition. The problem is that over time, it's discouraged by most schools, religious systems and families. It's rare that someone is taught and encouraged from birth to trust and love themselves completely and intuition is deeply tied in with trust and self-love.

Intuition is your body's connection to source consciousness. The only way to communicate with source consciousness is through the unconscious mind, not through your rational, conscious mind. The reason so many people doubt their intuition is because they allow their rational mind to run the show. Until you train your conscious, left-brain, rational mind to accept intuition, it's always going to get in your way by throwing up a wall of self-doubt, which is the opposite of self-love.

The key to successfully building your intuition is to love and trust yourself. Can you imagine loathing yourself, yet still trusting your intuition? Can you imagine trusting your intuition without trusting and loving everything else about yourself? It's harder to access source consciousness while doubting yourself, not trusting yourself or criticizing yourself.

A great way to train your conscious mind to accept your intuition is through a daily prayer and meditation practice. (See the next section for an easy way to set up a daily practice.) Prayer is calling out to God/source consciousness and meditation is how you receive a response. This call and response practice is subtle communication and unlike your usual conversation, which is why it takes dedication and persistence to master.

The subtle communication of prayer and meditation has a similar feel to intuitive messages, which is why the two work so well together. Whether you're in prayer, meditation or receiving intuitive messages, I invite you to pay attention to how your body feels. Since the unconscious mind is responsible for the body as well as for intuition, listening to subtle changes in your body is a great way to get accustomed to this new way of communicating.

For example, over time I've learned that I get a tightness and sick feeling in my stomach if something is off with the integrity around a situation or person I'm dealing with. This is clear communication from my unconscious-body-mind-intuition and it NEVER fails. It's always a sign that I need to pay close attention to what's happening around me. More than likely, you have similar body feelings or "gut instincts," but you may not be used to paying close attention and then acting on them.

I also recommend that you pay attention to your self-talk. If you're constantly criticizing yourself, how are you ever going to trust yourself? Look for ways you might be in criticism and self-doubt and do your best to eliminate them and refocus your thoughts on self-love. Both self-doubt and negative self-talk are subtle and insidious blocks to self-love and therefore, intuition.

Some of us have lived with self-doubt for so long, we don't even recognize that it's not who we really are. Self-doubt may show up as indecisiveness, needing the approval of others, lack of confidence or in other forms. If you become aware that you're in self-doubt, the first thing I invite you to do is congratulate yourself. Awareness is the first step toward change.

Once you're clear that you're feeling self-doubt, the easiest way to get out of it is to check in with your Human Energy System to see what it's communicating to you via feelings and sensations. When you decipher the messages from your Human Energy System, you can follow its guidance to get back on track. Get as clear as possible about what's bothering you and find ways to calm and center yourself. Prayer and meditation help. That's how easy it can be to trust and follow your intuition.

When it comes to negative self-talk, the first step out of it again, is to have awareness. Do your best to catch yourself in the middle of a negative thought and switch it to something positive.

One of my favorite things to say to get myself out of negative self-talk is, "I'm such a cute little human!"

For example:

NEGATIVE ME - "Wow that was a really dumb thing to do. What was I thinking?"

POSITIVE ME - "I'm such a cute little human! Oops - I forgot to take my perfect pill today."

I know, it sounds silly, but it works like a charm and the silliness immediately dissolves the tension that negative thoughts create in my body. I'm committed to trusting my intuition and I've learned over time how important it is to dissolve self-doubt and negative self-talk as soon as they pop up. This takes practice, so keep at it and eventually you'll be able to make the shift.

Here's a summary of the four-step process I teach in the Bloom Your Intuition course to maximize your innate intuitive gifts. You can use this process to speak to your Higher Power and you can also use it to communicate with the spirit teachers and the Divine Mother:

1. Set up a "Call and Response" practice.

Set an intention during your morning meditation. Communicate with God/source consciousness, the Divine Mother or a specific sacrament, and affirm that you're requesting a specific type of information. It can be anything at all, so don't limit yourself here. Have a clear intention and literally affirm that source consciousness will send you the information you desire. Grab your intuition journal and write down your intention. Even if it's the same multiple days in a row, write down the date and the issue.

FOR EXAMPLE: "God, I'm considering changing careers. I affirm that you'll show me a clear, unequivocal sign today for guidance toward my next step."

Don't expect the entire plan to be laid out for you in one fell swoop. Unfortunately, it doesn't always work that way.

2. Be receptive.

Once you've set an intention for the day, the next step is to pay attention. As you go through the day, be open and available for receiving signs. You can receive signs in any number of ways - from overheard conversations to bumper stickers, to dreams, reading something on the news, songs you hear, feelings or visions. Source consciousness is infinite and always communicating with you. If something catches your attention, assume it's intended for you.

3. Record the messages you receive.

Any time during the day (but definitely before you go to sleep at night), write down the messages you receive, even if they seem completely silly. This exercise specifically uses your conscious, rational mind, which is required for the motor movement of writing. The rational mind is also responsible for language, so when it sees the words on the page, it's completely engaged in the process.

A huge part of building and strengthening intuition is TRUSTING that it's working. To deeply TRUST your intuition, your conscious, rational mind needs to be on board, so it stops throwing out self-doubt to block you. Writing down the messages from God/source consciousness, the Divine Mother or a specific sacrament is a great way to get both hemispheres of your brain to trust each other.

Later, you can go back and review your progress. Everyone has their own psychic superpowers, so pay attention to the types of messages you're receiving. Believe everything and write it all down. Even if you don't immediately sense a solid connection between the responses you get from source consciousness and your original intention, don't give up. Keep going and the truth will eventually be revealed.

4. Act on the messages you receive!

Once you receive messages from your intuition and you've written them down, act on them. This is a fantastic way to get your conscious mind one-hundred-percent on board, and it's the best way to combat the self-doubt that inevitably pops up when you're doing this type of work. Even if you take action and it doesn't "seem" to go anywhere, simply acting on the intuitive guidance helps your unconscious mind know you're taking this practice seriously.

Now you have the unconscious mind involved with receiving the messages, the conscious mind involved with writing down information, and your whole brain experiencing the complete cycle of working with the messages as you take action on them. That's when resistance slips away and you're in easy flow working with your intuition.

The visions and insights from ceremony come straight from source consciousness through your unconscious mind, so this process is especially important when you're doing sacred medicine work. Recording your insights in your journal and then acting on them is the best way to honor the Divine Mother and make the most of your sacrament work.

Keep repeating these four steps until you've released resistance and you notice that on a regular basis you're moving from self-doubt to self-love as you increasingly trust your intuition.

How to Start a Prayer & Meditation Practice

If you haven't done it already, I highly recommend setting up a daily prayer and meditation practice. Prayer is simply communicating with and making requests to source consciousness and meditation is simply receiving information back. It's that straightforward. I know a lot of meditation lineages talk about emptying the mind, but I spend my meditation time receiving messages directly from my guides and ancestors, so my mind is definitely not empty and personally, I don't need it to be.

There's no "right" way to do meditation, but the meditation teachers I've learned from suggest keeping your daily practice in the morning, in a sacred space where you tap into and communicate with source consciousness in a way that resonates with you. At its simplest, a sacred space is an area used for the purposes of prayer, meditation and spiritual practices. I have some crystals, affirmations, an antique sound bowl, an incense burner and some sentimental items set up on an altar as my sacred space, but you're welcome to set up your sacred space however you'd like. As long as it's a place where you can feel calm and focused, it will work as a sacred space.

There are innumerable teachings available around meditation and prayer, but if you want to get started right away, experiment with this simple practice.

1. Set a quiet space in your house where you'll be undisturbed for

2. the entire time you plan to meditate. Turn off and put away all electronic devices and allow yourself to be fully present as best you can.
3. Start with the shielding practice from the beginning of the Resources section.
4. Next, here's an example of what you can say to start off your practice:

"I am one with my Higher Power, and I hereby affirm that I receive guidance from the light and only from the light. Today I'd like help with opening my intuitive channels. I affirm that I am worthy, and I deserve divine guidance on this issue."

That's the prayer part and you can affirm anything you desire. Next comes the meditation part.

4. Now that you've asked for assistance, sit quietly, breathing rhythmically until you receive an answer. And just like that, you're meditating! If your mind wanders (which it will), be kind and gently guide it back and center yourself in the meditative state again.

You can keep your prayer and meditation practice as simple as this or make it more elaborate. Just trust the process and release expectations about how it "should" work. If you're following these steps, you're doing it. Like anything else, prayer and meditation get better with practice.

Prayer and meditation work for building your intuition, integrating your lessons from sacred medicines, staying calm and focused and deepening your spiritual practice. There are multiple benefits from committing to a prayer and meditation practice, so I invite you to get started and see where it takes you.

Psychedelic Integration Coaching

If you need extra support with your sacred medicine work, consider working with a coach. As psychedelic medicine use becomes more widespread, more skilled practitioners are available to help you integrate your journeys into your daily life. Do an online search for "psychedelic integration coach" and see what comes up, either in-person in your local area or via online coaching.

Since this is a new area of expertise, you'll find people with a wide variety of experience and certifications. This isn't a regulated field, so my recommendation as always, is to trust your intuition. In today's world, most businesspeople have a website, so feel into what's presented online, what they say about themselves and their qualifications. Many practitioners will be at least willing to answer some questions via email and many offer a complimentary first session to see if it's a good fit for both of you.

Be aware of your budget ahead of time, but also remember that working with the least expensive person available is not necessarily the best option. Qualified people generally charge more for their time, so if money's an issue, you're better off doing fewer sessions with a highly qualified person than doing multiple sessions with someone who's inexpensive, but not very skilled or able to offer the deep assistance you may require.

Additionally, you can always work with me! As you know from reading this book, I have three-plus decades of experience studying human potential and spirituality and a decade of experience working with the psychedelic medicines. I also have several certifications, which you'll see in my bio in this book and on my website: www.inthedivine.com Please get in touch if you feel called to do integration work with me.

GLOSSARY OF TERMS

1st Chakra

According to Eastern philosophy, the body has multiple chakras, or wheels of energy that spin in specific locations of the body. This philosophy is thousands of years old and in fact the word "chakra" is the Sanskrit word for wheel.

Some perceive these wheels as two-dimensional energy centers located down the spinal column because that's how they're depicted in print. They're actually 3-D vortices of energy, extending in all directions, in multiple planes and corresponding to specific organ systems and specific life issues. The 1st/root chakra is associated with issues of security, safety, food, shelter and livelihood and corresponds to the organs of elimination.

Agave

A succulent plant that grows in hot, dry climates. The leaves and roots have medicinal uses, and the inner core or *"piña"* is the prime ingredient in both mezcal and tequila liquors.

Ayahuasca

An entheogenic tea originating in South America. It's produced from heating and concentrating two plants: the *Banisteriopsis* caapi vine and the leaves of the *Psychotria viridis* plant, which contains N,N-dimethyltryptamine (DMT).

Ayahuascero/a

A person trained in the art of brewing ayahuasca and setting up an ayahuasca ceremony. They may or may not also be a healer or curandero/a. (See that entry below.)

Bufo/Cane Toad

The bufo or cane toad is native to the Sonoran Desert. The *5-MeO-DMT* venom in its poison glands is much more powerful than the *N,N-Dimethyltryptamine* (DMT). The venom is milked from its glands and administered for health and spiritual purposes.

Cannabis

A flowering, leafy, sacred plant, present on the earth since the Miocene epoch (approximately 23 million to 5 million years ago). It's been used as medicine, as an aphrodisiac and for religious and divinatory purposes since long before recorded history.

Ceremony
A formal, ritualistic series of acts for a certain event. In many but not all indigenous lineages, the psychedelic medicines are consumed in ceremonial settings.

Cosmorgasmic Energy
Orgasmically charged, sexual and cosmic energy. It's divine creation energy and the pure root of existence, which is translated through you when your body is vibrating at a heightened state, under the influence of sacred medicines. Cosmorgasmic energy is the most powerful energy on the planet and a pathway to higher consciousness.

Curandero/a
A person who is a trained healer, working with ayahuasca and/or other sacred medicines as a means for physical, mental and spiritual healing. A curandero/a may or may not also be an ayahuascero/a (person who brews ayahuasca).

Damiana

A shrub that produces small yellow flowers, it's native to parts of Texas, Mexico, Central America, South America and the Caribbean. The leaves and flowers of damiana, *Turnera diffusa*, have been used for centuries and possibly before recorded history as an aphrodisiac, heart-opener and bladder tonic, among other medicinal uses.

Divine Mother / Grandmother

Ayahuasca is often called "Grandmother" or the "Divine Mother" because She is the spirit within many sacraments. She is the voice of the earth, Pachamama, and the consciousness of the planet.

Just as all human life begins as female and then splits into genders, She is prime, source life code, expressing itself as the primordial feminine. She holds the wisdom of the ages, and so She has been historically perceived as an ancient wise woman. Indigenous cultures believe that all on the earth are Her children, and She communicates with us directly through the psychedelic medicines.

DMT

N,N-Dimethyltryptamine (DMT) is a psychoactive (affecting the mind) molecule in some sacred medicines, which is also present in the brain and throughout the body. Although there have been many scientific experiments around ayahuasca, other medicines and DMT, no one knows the complete truth of exactly how they link with the brain.

DMT is one of the substances responsible for the colors, lights, geometrical patterns and other visions one sees when under the influence of sacred medicines.

Entheogen

An entheogen is a psychoactive substance that allows one to experience a connection to a higher power. It comes from the Greek word *éntheos*, meaning "inspired by god." I use entheogen here to differentiate sacred medicine work from the use of these spirit teachers recreationally as hallucinogenics, to "party" and be high.

Facilitator

A person who sets up space for a sacred medicine ceremony and manages the participants. A facilitator may or may not also be a curandero/a or shaman.

Gaia

The primordial Greek earth goddess and also a hypothesis that all living organisms on earth are part of a greater organism and work together synergistically to maintain the ecological balance of earth.

Huachuma

A tall, fast-growing, almost spineless cactus, *Echinopsis pachanoi* is native to the Andes mountains and is also cultivated in other parts of the world. It's mildly psychoactive (affecting the brain) and an ancient and revered spirit teacher and entheogen, commonly referred to as "Grandfather," in contrast to the "Grandmother" spirit within ayahuasca.

Human Energy System

The concept that the human body is less a solid structure, a noun; and more of a verb - an interdimensional system that's in constant flux and flow. The Human Energy System is an approach to the body with an understanding that it's influenced by time, space, planetary bodies, the past, present, future, and emotions.

The sacred medicines offer healing on multiple levels, which is why it's helpful to take the Human Energy System into account as one continues with sacred medicine work.

Iboga

An African shrub used with a long history of use for medicine and in rituals. It contains indole alkaloids and is used as a stimulant, aphrodisiac and hallucinogen. It's particularly noted for its success in healing addiction.

Icaros

Traditional indigenous songs used specifically to facilitate healing and expansion in sacred medicine circles. Most true *icaros* are given to a shaman directly by the sacraments themselves.

Interdimensional

Existing or pertaining to two or more dimensions. The spirits of the spirit teachers exist in a dimension other than the 3-D reality we live in. Psychedelic medicine experiences feel "otherworldly," because they're literally in "other worlds" or other dimensions.

Kambo Frog
A type of tree frog native to the Amazon. Its secretions contain bioactive peptides that create a purgative effect in the body.

Medicine
Substances that are ingested to alter consciousness and receive interdimensional wisdom. Also called, "psychedelics," "sacred medicine," or "sacrament."

Medicine Circle
The name for a group of people coming together one time in a ceremony to receive sacred medicines. It also refers to a particular lineage that holds sacred medicine ceremonies on a regular basis.

Pachamama
Similar to Gaia, above, Pachamama is a Mother Earth deity of the indigenous people of the Andes. She is often referred to in the context of sustainability and environmentalism.

Peyote
A small, round, slow growing ground cactus entheogen, *Lophophora williamsii* has been used for religious,

ceremonial and healing purposes by indigenous peoples for thousands of years. It's native to Mexico and Southern Texas.

Plant Medicine: See medicine, above.
Psilocybin

An entheogenic compound occurring in upwards of 200 different species of fungi. Imagery found in multiple archaeology sites across the globe show that entheogenic mushrooms have been used and revered since before recorded history.

Sacrament

See medicine, above.

ACKNOWLEDGEMENTS

I give reverent thanks to all the sacred medicines who've guided me over the last years, especially huachuma who has been the project manager for this book. My life has been permanently altered by the changes you've brought, and I'm honored to channel your wisdom to whomever is open to it.

I'm forever grateful to my many grandmothers on the other side, including Mariana Valenzuela, Alcadia Davila, Olivia Arévalo and of course my own mother, Isabelle Schlee, now also a grandmother in the light.

Thank you to my medicine sisters who helped me edit and improve this book: Vivian Lauderdale, Seema Seraj, and my dear friend Emilee Amara.

A special thank you to my calm and kind spiritual mentor, Amanda Romania. Your wisdom shone a light on this path when I needed it the most.

Thank you to all the souls I've encountered in medicine ceremonies. Your reflections, questions and insights form the basis of this book.

Deep gratitude to all the medicine facilitators I've met. Your gifts of time, love, energy and resources have expanded my life and the lives of so many. You have one of the hardest jobs on the planet and I celebrate your courage and dedication. May you continue to grow and joyfully serve those who need the sacred medicines.

Blessings, love and hugs to my mentor, the great healer Ariel Goin. Thank you for the most profound healings of my life and for being my mirror and teaching me about Oneness.

To my daughter Phoenix on the other side, thank you for choosing me.

Finally, unconditional love and gratitude to my son, Joaquín. You are everything to me and you give my life meaning. I'm honored to be your mother and guide.

Much love to all.

AUTHOR BIOGRAPHY

T. S. Valenzuela has studied spirituality, personal growth and human potential since the mid-1980s and has been working with sacred plant medicines since 2012. She is a biohacker, psychic, medium and student of sacred sexuality.

She's a veteran of the U.S. Army and earned her degree in Creative Writing/Poetry from San Francisco State University. Theresa is a certified NLP trainer, hypnotherapist, Time Line Therapy™ practitioner, psychedelic integration coach, reiki master, certified sex, love and relationships coach and certified teacher of female ejaculation and the G-spot.

She has extensive experience with transformation through grief and loss and has done voluminous research on women's health, relationships, communication, nutrition and the modern food supply.

When she's not writing, you can find her eating dark chocolate (but trying not to), sewing, pondering the mysteries of the cosmos and hosting the Orange County, CA Psychedelic Integration Group on www.meetup.com

You can connect with her for speaking engagements, coaching and her latest projects at hello@inthedivine.com, on her website www.inthedivine.com, at her Etsy Shop: BeInTheDivine, and on Instagram, TikTok and Pinterest: @beinthedivine

Made in the USA
Middletown, DE
22 August 2022